CONFESSIONS
of a CAFETERIA
CATHOLIC

CONFESSIONS
of a CAFETERIA
CATHOLIC

Richard Phillips

Library of Congress Control Number: 2012906295
ISBN: Hardcover   978-1-4691-9621-3
                   Softcover   978-1-4691-9620-6
                   Ebook   978-1-4691-9622-0

This book was printed in the United States of America.

To order additional copies of this book, contact:
Xlibris Corporation
1-888-795-4274
www.Xlibris.com
Orders@Xlibris.com
114827

Contents

To Ellen and the rest of my family.
For your support, encouragement and inspiration for this work.

For Mom.
You may not have agreed with all contained herein, but your
example as a Catholic-Christian made me who I am today.

And To Joe
For the gentle nudge that gave me the confidence to pursue a dream.

*   *   *

Confessions of a Cafeteria Catholic

Following are thoughts concerning the faith of a cradle Catholic who has seen some things that are spiritually moving and spiritually destructive in the Roman Catholic Church during the course of a lifetime. This is not intended to be an exhortation to other Catholics to change how they feel about their Church or to challenge their faith (two separate things.) It is not intended to be a theological treatise or some new catechism. If some find thoughts here that strike a chord of familiarity in their own conscience, it is because they are not alone in their search for God. From where I stand, that would be a satisfying result, as it has seemed like a lonely journey at times for me. A search for one's faith is an intensely personal one, wading through the lessons learned from the nuns and teachers as young people, the wounds experienced at the hands of men and women of the Church and finding solace in a faith that is at once mostly Catholic yet ultimately personal. It takes time, a lifetime, to examine what it is that we believe, who it is that we are, what our relationship is with God. And those examinations can only come from an adult view of all that it is that we have learned and experienced during that lifetime, what it is that we agree with and that with which we do not. These are thoughts, questions, observations, criticisms and in some cases condemnations. But they are my own. I speak for no one else.

By way of introduction, I was born and raised a Catholic in a small town in Nebraska. I spent two and a half years in a minor seminary studying for the priesthood, but at too young an age. I married a Lutheran and raised my kids as Lutheran. At one time I thought of leaving the Church but decided against it. I have been away from the Church for extended periods of time for one reason or another during my life, but have always returned. As I have aged I have been more and more inclined to consider my faith and how it relates to Catholicism. These are musings on some topics that at the time captured my interest and caused me to write them down. It has been my inclination to write down my thoughts in an attempt to organize them and to make them coherent for me. This allows me to move on to other considerations, whereas otherwise I would have these thoughts rolling around in my mind and coming to no satisfactory conclusion. There is no real consistent thread between any of the chapters contained herein, as they were written individually with no goal toward organizing them into a cohesive unit. But after some time and re-readings it occurred to me that they are, in fact, a unit—a unit that may be of interest to someone else. If you find it so, I am happy. If not they have served to formulate a sense of what my faith consists of and who it is that I am at this stage in my life, and that is what they were intended to be to begin with. But life is an ongoing, ever-evolving journey, so this may not be the end of my faith story. In fact it most certainly will not be. Things and people who enter my life will undoubtedly have an impact on that story and necessarily change it to some degree. In fact I am currently involved in a study with a man who will certainly cause me to re-examine what I think about certain aspects of my faith. But in looking back at a lifetime of change in my feelings and opinions about life and faith, I am convinced that that is a good thing. There is always a positive result that comes from examining one's position on any number of life's issues, in keeping one's mind open to other possibilities and new revelations. That has been the journey of mankind's evolution since the beginning, looking at the same things and seeing different views of the same idea and coming to a new clarity based on experience and a fuller knowledge of the topic as the result of new insights gained along the way.

I guess in considering the thoughts contained here it has more to do with me and my own perspective of life than of any one established religious institution, Catholic or otherwise. That is perhaps the goal of all men and women who strive to find themselves and their God while facing the joys and challenges of life, trying to find the faith that keeps them on the path of discovering who they are and what they believe. Pride and despair could cause that path to become obscured without a faith in a Creator who wants us back home with Him again. We have all been through both, hopefully finding that neither is the way to be honest about who we are, what we believe and who it is that we believe in. But it has become clear to me that there are as many paths to that goal as there are individuals trying to attain it. That, too, is a good thing. We must, each of us, find our own way. That does not give us permission to condemn anyone else's attempts, but rather to simply acknowledge that we are all following different maps. Our goals are the same, but how we arrive is as individual as our personalities are, as our experiences have been and who has had influence on us during the course of a lifetime. The goal is salvation. The way to salvation is between us and God.

*   *   *

Reflections On
Faith and Morality

1

Hiding Myself

My wife suggested the other day that I tried to keep myself private. I thought about this for awhile and decided that she isn't entirely correct. There are aspects of me that I do keep private, but it has more to do with personal perspectives on topics of importance to me, and a sense that revealing some of these perspectives to others would serve no good purpose. Anyone who knows me knows that I don't have a problem expressing an opinion if I feel strongly about something, so the idea that I would try to hide myself from the outside world isn't an accurate description of who I am. I do feel that at a certain point in our aging process we arrive at a time when we feel more confident in who we are as individuals, what our identities are. As young people, teens and twenties and even thirties, we try very hard to prove to others who we are without really coming to any personal recognition as to what that means. We may know who or what we'd like to be, or at least who or what we'd like others to think we are, but it takes a certain amount of maturing and introspection to come to some realization as to who we really are. Sometimes that is a humbling realization, sometimes a satisfying one, hopefully an honest one. At a point in our lives we realize that certain things that we considered very important as younger persons aren't nearly as important as we once thought. That certain things to which we didn't attribute much importance are important to our identity, who we really are. We accept the fact that there are certain ambitions that we probably will never realize, either because we don't have what it takes to accomplish those ambitions or that the importance of accomplishment is less so than we earlier thought. There are some things that we would do as a young person that at a later stage of life maybe aren't even desirable. Attitudes toward life evolve with age and life experience and, hopefully, an acquisition of some level of wisdom. We see our mortality as more of a reality, not just something theoretical that we don't really believe will happen to us in our immortal youth. We have a more realistic idea of what we believe, what's important and what's not. My role as father and grandfather is different than when my kids were young and depending on me for different things than they do now. Now my advice is sought rather than endured, my experience is appreciated rather than questioned. The number of years I've breathed on this earth gives me something they now consider valuable given their own limited number of years.

I see my faith as more personal and more real than I did as a younger man. When I was very young it was very important to me, but not very real. It was someone else's faith, my parents', my minister's, but not yet really my own. It has taken a journey of many years and many personal realizations and religious crises to accept the faith I have now as my own and the importance it has in my life. Some may call me a cafeteria Catholic because of my rejection of certain aspects of Roman Catholicism, and I don't deny that as an apt description of who I am, but I don't apologize for it, either. My faith is based on some principles that I learned growing up, adjusted by a realization that those principles may be affected by other people and finally attuned to my own grasp of what is real for me personally. I don't try to impose my faith on others, and I appreciate it when others don't try to change mine. Some may find this offensive or even immoral, but immorality for me would be claiming to believe something that I don't. More than at any time in my life my faith is a very important aspect of who it is that I am. My wife comes from a different religious heritage than I do, and I have realized that she, too, has found increasing importance in something faithful. Our differences have become more significant since we were younger, and as a result could be a source of tension in our marriage. As a result we don't discuss our differences in any depth, and as a result, because of their relative importance in our lives, some silence has developed in our relationship. I don't think it's damaging to our marriage, but it does change it somewhat. Even if we had both come from the same religious traditions, our personal experiences would likely have changed what our current faiths are at this point in our lives, not to the same degree perhaps, but different nevertheless.

Faith wasn't what I had planned to write about in this essay, but it points to the importance it holds in my life. However it may just be an example of how our lives evolve over time. Our attitudes about politics, religion, race, financial security, what position our children and grandchildren now hold in our lives—all these things and more have changed given the years we have spent together, the experiences we've shared and, yes, even the years we spent apart when we were very young. Like all people of our age we are different than we once were, hopefully for the better. It may be a reason for the discomfort in openly discussing those private matters within us that we once proclaimed from the mountaintops. We no longer find it necessary to prove to others who we are. We are now comfortable with our identities and all that that entails. Privacy, yes, even silence, about these things is now okay for us. For those around us, those who have grown up and grown older with us, it may be troubling, as if something is wrong or that we have changed fundamentally in our relationships. This isn't necessarily true, at least I don't think so in my case. Silence and a certain amount of privacy simply means contentment with who I have become. I have arrived at a point that gives me some security as to what's real in my life, which ambitions are still realistic, which ones I may abandon without guilt or remorse. We are not at the end of the road yet, but we can see the signs for the exit ramp ahead, and it's not something to panic over. We have some time yet (we think) to accomplish a few things, to see some of the results of our efforts come to fruition, to make some friends and to be a friend to some. At this point that's not a bad goal. It takes a load off our shoulders and gives the twilight years some sense of rocking chair comfort. I never thought that day would come, but it's not a bad prize for a race run. I look forward to being someone my grandchildren will remember with some wistfulness after I'm gone, someone my kids will appreciate one day, someone my wife will miss if I go before her and someone a friend will smile at the thought of occasionally. That would be a life well lived, and silence about my thoughts regarding that life is allowed.

2

Family Faith

There was a time in our not-too-distant past when people who married did so within their own faith, or if they didn't, one party converted to the other's faith in an attempt to raise their children with a united family religious identity. Over the past few decades that practice has faded. Perhaps it has to do with a less important role religion has taken in the lives of many. Perhaps it has been more a reflection of a diminishing dedication to any formal personal philosophy, religious or otherwise. It may be that the youth of the sixties and seventies have seen a departure from the faith of their parents as a form of rebellion against the status quo, or a declaration of independence from established religion and its importance in raising a family. It may also be just the opposite. It may be that parents of today and the recent past have decided that one's personal faith is more important than the need to pass a single religious practice down to children from both parents. It may be that a respect for different points of view, including religious ones, is seen by parents as an important aspect of educating their children regarding differing backgrounds and viewpoints on many of life's issues as adults. That this is an important part of their responsibility as a parent to hand on to their children. The question then becomes, under which parent's faith are the children to be raised? Another consideration is whether or not either parent has a faith strong enough that it is important to pass any faith down to the next generation, or if no faith at all is preferable. Regardless of how that decision is made between two people, the important thing is to do it with respect for the faith not shared by the children and for the parent holding that faith, as well for those outside the family circle who hold to a faith different from their own. It should be considered to be a very important decision, made by both parents before the children become old enough to recognize any potential disagreement between the parents as to how to decide the matter.

Weekly church attendance is in decline nationwide, and thus the importance of faith is diminished in the eyes of the children by the example of the parents. This may not be the intention of the parents, but the lesson is learned, nevertheless. This lesson affects many other attempts at important aspects of childrearing. Why should the children be convinced of the value of honesty and honor and respect for others—why should they be convinced that any moral code holds importance in their lives if this lesson is part of their upbringing? The increase of crime and the decrease of a sense of consequence for actions taken by young people today may very well be a direct result of this lesson learned. Ultimately any moral compass is the result of some religious background. Without religion and a faith in a Supreme Being who expects living rightly, why should anyone decide to behave with any moral dimension to his or her life? There are occasions that cause an adult to choose not to participate in organized religion, but inconvenience should not be one of those reasons. Participation should be taught not only as a moral responsibility but as a gift not to be taken lightly. Many over the course of history have sacrificed their lives for the right to worship. To not participate because of hangover, late night activity or just because it's too far to drive teaches the young that it's just not that important. An adult's decision to not participate may be the result of disillusionment or principle or something else, but that decision should be reserved for the adult, not the child. And to make that decision lightly when children are watching and learning is to not take seriously one's responsibility for raising a good, morally sound child to a good, morally sound adult.

3

Faith

I didn't mean to stir up the emotions expressed in your response to my letter, but I'm not surprised that I did. I told you once that I didn't think that you could really abandon the faith of your childhood, because it is part of your identity, part of who it is that you are. Having said that, I can also say that some of the people I've known in my life are converts and are as faithful to their new faith (or more so) than they had been to their original faith. Some converted to accommodate the demands of my Church that married couples in the Catholic Church must both be Catholic. That was the rule back in the early days of my life and before. Grandma's sister-in-law is a convert, and she is as faithful as Grandma was, even after her husband, Grandma's brother, died and the need to be Catholic no longer existed. Grandma's other brother converted to Lutheranism for the same reason. I have never discussed their religious decisions with either of them to find out how they felt about their decisions long-term, but they have held onto their new faiths longer than I've had my own. Rick is another example, a former Catholic who became a Lutheran minister, and one of the most laudable and faithful men I've ever met.

Part of the problem in determining what your faith really is as an adult is that, like all forms of education, most of the teachers you encounter believe completely in what they teach, and think that their students should take everything that's being taught as "gospel." From Sunday school on the teachers are chosen for their devotion to the faith of the Church and for a confidence that they will teach their lessons as they learned them. When you're five years old and learning about God how can you doubt an adult teacher's version of the faith? As you approach Confirmation, those lessons are reinforced and as an older student, wanting to be part of the Church of your parents, you have no reason to doubt or question what you've been taught. It's only as a young adult that you begin to wonder. Sometimes it's about independence, sometimes about rebellion, sometimes just a more adult look at all you've been exposed to as a child. I think that in spite of most of the questions asked by those young adults, for whatever reason they questioned, most of the time they find their way back to the faith of their childhood. But now, as the result of an adult examination, it becomes their own faith, not just their parents' faith. But as I've noted that's not always the way it turns out.

There are "good Lutheran responses" and "good Catholic responses", all learned as a child from teachers who had formidable influence over their charges. I also know about the loyalty you have for Mom's beliefs, and how it may affect your relationship with her if you choose something she feels strongly about. Thus the loneliness. What it boils down to, I think, is that you are now at a point in your life that you can examine with maturity what it is you agree with and what it is you disagree with about your faith. What is it that's important to you? You also have the responsibility to guide your kids down whatever path you choose. Welcome to parenthood! In any event, the aspects of heart and mind are difficult to separate, but in order to have something that belongs to you, especially something as important as what your faith is, it's at least necessary to examine that faith carefully. Faith in God is essentially different than the Lutheran faith, or the Catholic faith, or Islam or Hari Krishna or whatever. They are all just methods of finding God. Finding your God is the most important part of the examination. Our identity changes and evolves throughout our lives. There is only so much truth to the saying, "We are who we are." We are who we become as the result of the influences in our lives, both good and bad, and unfortunately religion has aspects of both. As I've gotten older these issues seem to occupy more and more of my thoughts, and the only way for me to resolve them in my mind is to write it down. It allows me to formulate a coherent idea about what is going on in my mind, and to come to conclusions (hopefully) about what that entails. Much of it Grandma probably wouldn't have approved of when she was here. That may not be the case now. At any rate I'm still trying to find out what it is that I believe in. Good luck, and know that I'm always here. I love you.

4

A Child's Faith

We went to church yesterday and then went to eat afterward. During our meal we discussed your family's apparent lack of any real commitment to attending church or having the kids involved in Sunday School. That bothers both of us. The kids are old enough to learn the importance (or lack thereof) of their parents' faith lives. I don't know the reasons as to why you don't have such a commitment. But you know (or should know) that when you guys became parents you accepted the responsibility to raise your kids with a healthy, positive attitude toward life and all that that entails. They are very obviously happy and healthy physically, but an important part of their education has to do with a faith. I know it's not always convenient to get everybody up for church on Sunday morning, but convenience shouldn't be the prerequisite for the things you teach your kids. They learn whether you make it important in their lives (and yours) or not. The question is what exactly are they learning when you don't make religion a priority? You can be assured that they are learning something. You should have a relatively easy time choosing a faith community to be a part of, unlike Mom and I did. But we did, and we raised you kids with a faith. At the time it was our faith, (Mom's denomination, but our faith.) Whether that is still the faith you have is an adult decision the two of you need to make, but make it. If you don't teach your kids that faith is important pretty quickly, we're concerned that before you know it you'll have kids with no faith at all. That concerns us. As your parents we still feel the responsibility to make our feelings known. Those responsibilities evolve as your kids become older, but they don't go away. I can only assume that this is inertia on your parts, and that's not how a parent should exercise his or her responsibilities. It is important.

5

Christmas

It's Christmas and I've been thinking about the circumstances surrounding the original Christmas. Things can't have been as rosy as they've been portrayed in art and literature and music over the centuries. Mary may have been about 14 years old and pregnant and a virgin. That had to be hard to take in for a girl of virtue, part of a people who had been waiting for a messiah for a very long time. Joseph had to take the word of an angel that Mary had not been leading a loose lifestyle. An angel. How many of us have had an angel appear to us and speak to us, especially speaking of something as personal as that? Then there was the trip from Nazareth to Bethlehem. No interstates back then, and the mode of transportation was not exactly suitable for a girl pregnant and nearing her due date. Riding on the back of a donkey over hills and rocks and fording streams for 113 kilometers. That's a trip. Then they arrive and no lodging is available, except for a cave that livestock use for shelter. Now comes the labor and delivery. There is no midwife. Neither Mary nor Joseph have ever been through this experience before. We've all seen the depiction of birth on television and movies, and some of us have even been in the delivery room of a nice, clean, sterile hospital with doctors and nurses dressed in white, arms raised in the air to preserve their sterility, soft music playing in the background to keep mom and dad at ease. Lots of clean sheets and warm lights and people doing everything correctly to see to it that the new baby is born safely and checked over after the birth to see that everything is as it should be. Now back to the cave. The smell of old hay and manure, no clean sheets, no experts to assist in the order of things, no music playing, no spinal block, no caesarian sections, no crib, no clean water to clean the Baby in—just two inexperienced, tired, soon-to-be parents trying to fumble through this "natural" experience. Does Joseph help in the delivery or does he stand outside worrying while Mary does it alone? Okay, the Baby is here, dried off with something and breathing on His own. What to do with Him? They decide to use a manger—a feeding trough for the cattle and sheep, maybe with some hay in the bottom to make it more comfortable, maybe the hay covered with a coat so as to be not so scratchy.

Then comes the music. Do angelic choirs sing for the multitudes or just for the new family? Do the "hosannahs" and the "hallelujahs" from the heavens rouse the sleeping town of Bethlehem or just the shepherds? And speaking of the shepherds, are they welcomed with open arms in the midst of the ordeal of the delivery they've just been through, or were they intruders on a night when they just wanted to get some sleep or to revel in the presence of their new Baby? All these things have been seen through rose-colored lenses over time by people who were never there.

I don't mean to imply that this wasn't a glorious event for all concerned, because it was—the most glorious event in human history to that point. But in real human terms, how was it for the people involved? How was it for that 14 year-old girl, tired and dirty from a very long, hard journey. How was it for a new husband and father, still nervous about what his responsibilities would be for his wife and son? What were they to expect and what would their experiences be as the parents of a Messiah? Imagine yourself in their position, knowing the nervousness at the birth of your own child. From the songs written and the stories told about that first Christmas things were clean and bright and comfortable. In the reality of the day it probably was anything but.

Merry Christmas, and thank God for two inexperienced people who took the word of angels and did something remarkable, bringing to life the prophesies of old and starting something for the world the likes of which we'd never seen, changing the course of humankind for all time, starting a tradition of families (shepherds, wise men, aunts, uncles, children and grandchildren) getting together to celebrate something both "natural" and anything but. Hallelujah.

6

A Christmas Story

Once upon a time, there was a young married couple who were going to have a baby—their first baby. They were excited about having a new baby in their home, playing with him. But they were nervous, too. Neither of them knew much about having a baby, and doctors and hospitals hadn't really been invented yet. In those days there was usually some lady called a "midwife" who would be called to your home when the baby was about to be born to help with the birth. Maybe they had a lady picked out already or maybe not. We don't know. But before they could have the baby, the Emperor told everybody that he wanted to know how many people there were in the world, so he wanted to count them all. Every man was supposed to go to his home town with his family to be counted, even if you now lived a long way away from your hometown, you had to travel to get there. So the husband took his wife and started off to his hometown, which was a long way from where they lived now. The problem was that this was going to be a very difficult trip, because the roads weren't very good and they didn't have a car, only a donkey for his wife to ride on. He would have to walk, leading the donkey. Now this was a pretty long trip. It would be like walking from Sidney to Wyoming—even farther than that. There weren't many towns along the way to stop to rest, no motels, no restaurants, no bathrooms. They would have to carry food and water for themselves, and stop every so often to let the donkey eat and drink and rest. They probably had to carry some kind of shelter in case it rained, and blankets to cover with at night, because this trip would take more than just one day. Now remember, the wife was going to have a baby, so she probably wasn't very comfortable riding on that donkey with a big belly, hoping the baby didn't decide to be born while they were traveling.

Finally they arrived at Joseph's hometown (did I tell you that his name was Joseph?) And his wife's name was Mary. She was pretty young. Nowadays she might only be in junior high or maybe a freshman in high school. Anyway, when they got to the town, Bethlehem was the name of the town, they found out that there were a lot of other people who were supposed to be counted who had gotten there before them, and they had filled up all the hotel rooms. There wasn't any place to stay. Some old farmer who lived in Bethlehem told them they could stay in his barn if they wanted to, but it wasn't a very big barn and it was out in the country. What else could they do? So Joseph helped Mary get back on the donkey and they went looking for the barn. When they found it out in the country, they discovered that it really wasn't a very big barn, more like a little cave in the side of a hill. But it was dry and the cows and sheep were friendly, so they unpacked and decided to get some rest. But guess what. The baby decided it was time to be born. But there wasn't any midwife to help, and it certainly wasn't very clean in that old barn and it was kind of smelly. But it was dry and the cows and sheep helped keep it kind of warm in there. So it happened. The baby was born in a barn. It wasn't very fancy, there were no beds and no crib for the new baby. So they used a manger, which is kind of a feed trough that the cows and sheep used to eat their hay in. But with some hay in the manger, and a coat over the hay it was probably comfortable for the baby (babies are pretty small and don't take up much room.) Maybe the cows and the sheep came over to have some supper and wondered what a baby was doing in their manger, but as I said, they were friendly so they probably didn't mind eating around him. Oh yeah, it was a baby boy.

And out in the fields there were some other farmers, called shepherds, who were watching their sheep to keep the wolves and coyotes from eating them at night, and to keep rustlers from stealing them. And you know what? Up in the sky they saw an angel! He told them about the baby being born in the stable and that they should go check it out. And then a whole bunch of other angels showed up in the sky (angels can fly, you know) and they sang songs about the baby. So the shepherds went to the barn to see this baby that the angels had been singing about. It was pretty cool. And then three camels showed up outside with some important-looking guys riding them. They said they were kings, wise men from the East and that they had been following this star to find the baby. The shepherds hadn't noticed any star, so they went outside and looked, and sure enough this one bright star was shining its light right on the barn where they were. So they all went back in the barn and said "Hi!" to Mary and Joseph and the baby. The kings had brought some gifts for him, kind of birthday presents. They were pretty surprised that all this had happened out in this old barn, with only cows and sheep and shepherds and these three wise men to welcome him, instead of having the whole town of Bethlehem giving them their best room to sleep in, and their best midwife to help the baby being born, and maybe even the mayor giving a speech or something. If angels had sang songs about him, surely more people than just them would be there. But there weren't. It was only supposed to be them.

Mary and Joseph thought this was pretty strange that all these things were happening like this, and they had no idea what was going to happen next, but they had a new baby. And it was pretty exciting. Everybody was safe and warm and healthy, and they had even had a birthday party on the day he was born, complete with presents. How many new babies can say that? So after some time they went back home and watched the baby grow up. As he got older his father taught him how to be a carpenter, but he had more important things to do than that. He didn't live to be a very old man, but he lived long enough to be the most important man who ever lived. And Mary and Joseph remembered all that had happened on that night, in that stable, with the cows and the sheep and the shepherds and the wise men (and don't forget the angels!), and they remembered how special it was on that very first Christmas night.

The End

7

Christmas Benevolence

It has been suggested that this year, given the tight economy and everyone's budget crunch, that rather than exchange gifts within the family, we have a time when each couple or individual tell of some act of charity they have committed during the Christmas season. I have some trouble with this concept. Yes, it does give each of us a heartwarming moment to hear of one of our own doing good for someone in need, and if the children are present it gives them an example of what Christmas should be about—giving rather than receiving. These are good things, but I still have a problem. Charity should be a private matter. Doing good for someone in need is something we are directed to do, but bragging about it is not. I understand that "bragging" isn't exactly the right term, but our reward for doing good should be the satisfaction of doing what God wants us to do, not the admiration of our fellows. It should be between us and God. If we receive the adulation of our friends and family for benevolent works, then that is our reward. If that is the reward we seek, then our benevolence isn't so benevolent. Yes, the good is done no matter the reason, but I don't think the left hand should know what the right hand is doing. It gets back to the reason for Christmas, and for how we should live our lives every day. It is better to give than to receive. To give anonymously is better, in my opinion, than to receive praise for giving. I believe it has to do with our principles, with our character, with the way we live our lives and serve our God. If, as a photographer, I was paid for my work I shouldn't expect to receive any further compensation for that work when I reach Heaven. It isn't charity anymore if we have received some compensation for our works here on earth already, even if that compensation is only a smile of approval from a friend. We have then been paid. Maybe that's not a bad thing, as I said, especially if it provides an example to others as to how to live and how to treat those less fortunate than ourselves. And if we expect no further reward than that, then so be it. I guess it all depends on our motives for doing good. Do we do good for the benefit of others or for the benefit of ourselves? Do we do good to please God or to impress those around us? I guess it just depends on us. If the Rockefeller Foundation was named for Moses or St. Joseph or something, would it exist? Would Bill and Melinda Gates have started a foundation if their names had not been attached? Yes, institutions like these do a lot of good for a lot of people, but will the Rockefellers and the Gates' receive immortal recognition or have they already received their compensation because everyone who's interested knows of their benevolence? Perhaps the Rockefellers and the Gates' do other good anonymously in addition to their public displays of good works. If so their reward shall be great, but not for their foundations. Our own benevolence should be carried on in private, our charitable works anonymously. We know and God knows. That's enough.

Matthew said in his sixth chapter "Be careful that you don't do your charitable giving before men, to be seen by them, or else you will have no reward from your Father who is in heaven." On the other hand, Matthew also says to "Let your light shine before men, that they may see your good deeds and praise your Father in Heaven . . . ." Hmmm.

8

Evil

There was an editorial on NPR this weekend regarding the presence of evil in the world. It was a piece on the atrocities committed by so-called terrorists around the world in recent years against those with whom they disagree. Many who responded to the editorial denied the concept of "evil" in general, and against using the term to judge those who, in their opinion, may have felt justified in using murder to avenge perceived insults committed against them or against their kindred spirits. The piece was prompted by atrocities committed in India this past week against Westerners of any kind and against Jews. There was coverage on the Denver television news this weekend showing the reaction of fellow Jews to the murders of a young rabbi and his family who lived in Mumbai where the incidents took place. One man indicated that the proper response to such acts were "mitsvahs"—acts of kindness rather than revenge.

To deny the presence of evil in the world because it is an easy way out of having to deal with issues, or because "evil" is in the eye of the beholder is nonsense. Evil and good coexist in the world, whether we like it or not. To deny the existence of one is to deny the existence of the other, and to deny the existence of good in the world is a tragic way to look at life. Evil has been a reality since before the beginning of time, and has been part of our human existence since the beginning. There is no denying that some justify their actions as honorable for some higher cause, but to justify all actions with that same rationale takes away all responsibility for actions taken by anyone for any reason. Taking no responsibility for our actions is why our world is in the sad state that exists now. Good, too, has been part of our humanity since the beginning, but that is not to say that everything we do is good. We have the free will to do good or not. We have the free will to act responsibly with the welfare of our fellow humanity in mind or not. If we choose not, we must take responsibility for that choice, and if that means condemnation by the world and by God, then so be it. The fact that there are others in the world that may support and applaud those acts does not make those acts honorable, only that there are others in the world with the same evil in their hearts. Evil is a reality. The logical outcome of evil is more evil, eye for eye, tit for tat—revenge, more acts of evil, each act justified by some act committed against one by the other. There is no end to the cycle except the one advocated by those Jews in Denver—return evil with good. This is by no means an easy path to take, but if we are to minimize the evil in the world it must be done with good, not with more evil. Only by demonstrating our own willingness to demonstrate good rather than evil will our enemies find no justification for their own acts of evil.

9

Life and Darkness

Life is not inherently bad. We all have bad days, but life wasn't created as some macabre exercise to see how much we could take before we were rewarded in Heaven. Man wasn't created because God needed us, either for company or as subjects merely to worship and adore Him. He doesn't require the company of the human race for some big celestial, eternal party for His amusement. All that implies a fundamental flaw in His character, and if we believe Him to be omnipotent and perfect and whatever other adjectives we would place before His name, that implication is wrong. He got by without us just fine for eternity. I don't know what His exact reasons were for creating man. I've been taught that we were created in His image, with free will to obey His commands or not, and we failed. As a result of that failure we have bad days, some have bad lives. But that wasn't the reason for our creation, and life, in and of itself, is not dark. It's not perfect. Adam and Eve destroyed that perfection, and we have followed in their example. If they had not eaten the forbidden fruit we may have each had to pass our own test in our own time, maybe not. But the world and all that it contains was not created to be a dark, despairing place, merely for the temporal suffering of mankind. Yes, Heaven will be infinitely better, but this isn't hell, either.

To view life as dark, inherently dark, has more to do with one's attitude than with one's circumstance. There is no problem with looking forward to salvation, anticipating its rapture, but to view our existence here, now as some kind of punishment is to deny God's wisdom in our creation in the first place. There is joy to experience, satisfaction to feel here living on earth. One Man came to earth to share in our experience. He was born, lived in modest means and died. Maybe that was the only way to reconcile man to God, maybe not. But in any event He came to us as man, to live as we live, and He did so willingly. If life is dark and He is light, that constitutes a dichotomy between what He is and what He did. If He did bring light into a dark world, then our darkness disappeared 2000 years ago. Any darkness we feel now is of our own making, and in light of the salvation story, unnecessary. Our goal should be to dissipate the darkness in the world, to bring as much light into our existence as we are able, to share that light with others and to prove to the unbelievers that this is not an exercise in futility, that our God is a God of hope, not of vengeance. When we sing, plant a seed, write or do anything that demonstrates whatever gifts we have been given, it is for the glory of the One who created the world and to prove that our existence is indeed a measure of how we were created in His likeness. Cheer up, enjoy your life, your spouse, your kids, your grandkids, your dreams and ambitions. Life is not so dark that we can't just turn on the Light.

10

Forgiveness

Yesterday I heard someone say that, "The inability to forgive is a poison you take hoping someone else will die." It stopped me cold. In my experience the inability to forgive is perhaps the weakness most difficult to overcome for a human being, at least for this human being. The grudges I have carried over the years have caused me more pain and discomfort than any experience I can think of. And those few grievances that I have allowed to, or rather been allowed to, leave behind have brought me as much peace as any good thing I may have accomplished in my life. The inability to forgive is, in fact, a poison—a poison to the soul. We spend our lives learning about the teachings of Jesus, and His command to love one another, and to forgive one another, not seven times, but seventy times seven times. And yet we find it difficult, nearly impossible at times, to follow that admonition. I believe that the tendency to react to a perceived injustice, to seek revenge, to hold a grudge comes to us as children. I see babies swat at a hand they don't want interfering with them, I see toddlers seeking retribution when a toy is taken away, I see all ages sulking when they feel injured. These reactions may be momentary or they may be long-lasting. As adults those reactions don't really change, but are less overt, directed inward, held onto as passionately as any hate, and most of us have very long memories. If we decide that the injustice that is the cause of the feeling is serious enough, that inability to forgive may last for a very long time, and thus the poison affects our soul, our personality, our outlook on life. I see people whose entire existence is soured by divorce or other hardship. The negativity inherent in their day to day living affects everything they do, every life they touch. The longer it takes to find the ability to forgive, the harder it is to let it go, to regain a positive outlook. Without realizing it they create their own prison with bars of their own construction, holding them away from happiness without even recognizing its effect. It's said, "Love one another . . . ." and "Do unto others . . . ." In the abstract these things are things we strive for. In theory it's the natural thing to do. But in reality, in the real world of relationships with other people these sayings are anything but natural and easy. Unless we try. Unless we make it a constant practice, like exercise or diet, it won't take effect, and we won't find the antidote to the poison for ourselves. The inability to forgive is a poison we take, and the ability to find a way to overcome that inability will make us whole again.

11

Which Wolf To Feed

There is an old Cherokee fable.

> One evening, a grandfather was teaching his young grandson
> about the internal battle that each person faces.
> "There are two wolves struggling inside each of us," the old
> man said.
>
> "One wolf is vengefulness, anger, resentment, self-pity, fear.
> The other wolf is compassion, faithfulness, hope, truth, love."
>
> The grandson sat, thinking, then asked: "Which wolf wins,
> Grandfather?"
> His grandfather replied, "The one you feed."
> Each of us has to ask ourselves, which wolf will we feed?

This concept gives us cause to consider our attitudes toward life in general and our relationships with others in particular. We, each of us, have a tendency to feed the wrong wolf, whether because of our human nature or by attitudes learned from friends and family. There is a tendency to cultivate an attitude of suspicion, resentment, pessimism, self-pity, paranoia—you know the attitude. Nursing this state of mind causes argumentativeness, judgement of others, greed, a desire to seek revenge for perceived slights, despair and almost any other self-destructive persuasion we may be tempted to foster. If we fall into the temptation to feed these attitudes, it affects our entire outlook, our actions toward others, our happiness in general. We can become negative about all things, and without realizing it we fall deeper and deeper into a spiral of negativity about all things. I hear people bemoaning their relationships with family and friends, their health, sleeplessness, the unfairness of life in general and a universally sour attitude that causes most of those with whom they come into contact to avoid them, either consciously or subconsciously. They tend to complain about everything, they anger more quickly and for lesser reasons, they become strident in their attitudes about politics, religion, their personal philosophies, and they make it difficult for anyone to get near them. They isolate themselves, keeping others away because of distrust, fear or just a need to avoid the possibility of imminent pain resulting from disappointments that can never be avoided. After a time these attitudes become so ingrained that they become our personalities. We all face these temptations, and more often than not, succumb to them. We probably don't even recognize the traits associated with the personalities developed over a lifetime or over a moment. As I said, these are the tendencies we face. Like anything else it is up to us whether to feed this wolf or not.

Another choice we have is to cultivate an attitude of love, forgiveness, hope, satisfaction and openness. This attitude is more difficult to foster, less natural to maintain. The natural tendency is the first, and to succeed at fostering this other tendency requires painstaking attention, conscious denial of the other, practice, practice and more practice to remain open to others, willing to give of ourselves rather than bend to the suspicion that more will be taken from us than we give. We can be open to the opinions of others, even if we don't always agree with those opinions. We can have discussions, even debate without argument and resentment. We can try not to burden others with our own problems, and in the process of not dwelling on those problems they become less burdensome to us. The more we try to cultivate a positive attitude toward life in general, to feed the right wolf, it becomes easier, more natural, and our personalities come to reflect that positiveness making it easier for people to approach us. It's a choice that we make for ourselves, and it's a choice that must be made every day. But each day we choose to feed the right wolf, the easier it is to make that same choice the next day.

12

We Are All Different

P eace in our world assumes that we are all trying to live together without doing injustice to each other. This has been the goal of great men for millennia. We try to accommodate all people in that attempt, and in trying to do so we try to understand and correct the injustices that have been experienced by others in our world over time.

There is a misperception rampant that we can empathize with others for whom we have sympathy, understand what motivates someone who behaves in a manner out of the norm or justly criticize those whose philosophies differ from our own. We see people that have experienced a life different from ours and presume that we can rightly know what then causes certain behaviors and attitudes, and can have an enlightened knowledge of the world outside our own insular existence. This attitude is both presumptuous and naive, and does a disservice to others and prevents serious progress toward unifying segments of society in particular and humanity in general. It is impossible to have any idea what it's like to walk in someone else's shoes or to know what they think and how they process information given the reality of their own life experience. I can no more understand the reality of my own brother's world than I can a member of a group that has experienced prejudice among a majority population or a foreigner who has grown up under a different religious, political, ethnic, economic or ecological reality than I have. I cannot know how my position as the eldest in my family has affected the youngest, or how my parents' expectations of me were different from those they had of my brothers and sisters. I don't know how the year I was born or my gender, how my family's birth order or the friends I knew growing up, how real or imagined slights at the hands of others make my attitudes different than those of my siblings. And we are the closest thing to similar that we will know as humans. To presume that I can understand the difference between growing up as a white middle class Catholic in a small town in Nebraska and that of growing up as a black lower class Protestant or Jew or Muslim or atheist in a city ghetto because I read some books or took some classes is ludicrous. To assume that I am broadminded enough to know these things or to even have an informed opinion about them is inane. I can't know, for instance, how my studying for the priesthood when I was 14 has affected my attitudes toward the Catholic church or toward life in general compared to what it may have been had I stayed home and continued going to class with the same people with whom I went to elementary school. I can't know if one of my younger siblings was affected, either positively or negatively, by their association with me, how my parents affected me differently than they affected the rest of the family, how my marriage to the woman I wed made me different than the man I may have become had I married someone else or had not married at all. Each decision we make, every turn we take in life's road, everyone we meet on that journey changes us. So how can we claim to understand the effects life has had on others, either those close to us or those of whom we have no real knowledge? There are those who have made careers out of claiming to have some insight into the psychology of victims. We cannot offer understanding, and any attempt to do so is probably insulting to those victims. All we can do is offer an ear or a shoulder and an interest in their story. We can tell them our own stories and try to find some common ground where we can both be safe to listen and offer encouragement. Unity doesn't come from pretending to know what we cannot know. It comes from recognizing that we are each of us different, with different stories to tell, different life experiences, different pains and sorrows and joys to share—or not to share. Unity also accommodates the need for privacy and separation while remaining part of the human family. Unity acknowledges that there will be some whose stories make us uncomfortable, some whose stories we will never fully understand as well as stories with which we can find relationship, because, real or not, they remind us of something familiar in our own stories. Peace in our world comes from proximity without the fear of harm. It comes from being willing to listen and relate or to be there just in case. If we can accept our differences without judgment, if we can accept the fact that there is anger in the world for things over which we have no control and if we try to find common ground with those around us, maybe the goal of unity is possible.

13

The Shack

I just finished reading a novel called "The Shack". It was about a man who had lost his young daughter to a serial killer three years earlier, and a summons by God to come back to "the shack" where evidence of her murder had been discovered. The story is of a man's faith restored, finding the ability to forgive, a discovery of what God's relationship with the world really is and taking that information back to family and friends to try to explain his experience without sounding crazy. There has been a lot of interest in the way the story of God has been revealed in this book, either very positive or very negative. There is very little gray area in the opinions of those who have read the book and responded to the blog about the story. I get the feeling that the ones who are positively impressed with the story are those whose idea of the deity is less structured or bound by the teachings of an institutional religious denomination. Those negatively impressed seem to be threatened by any notion that goes against the security of the "facts" about God taught in Sunday School or Catechism, to the point that some even question its Christian roots in spite of the depiction of a Trinity of Father, Son and Spirit and a history of human birth and death of the Son.

Much of what I read I was able to accept readily, some of it only with some further thought about its implications and also some that I find I can either take or leave. Ultimately it is, in fact, a novel, a work of fiction, not an attempt to be a theological treatise. It does not attempt to convince anyone that this is the ultimate truth and that it is necessary to buy into it lock, stock and barrel. I find it to be a very interesting story of a God of which we have little real knowledge that puts a different slant on Him, on us, on His relationship with us and our relationship with Him, as well as an attempt to show a different way of relating to those around us here on earth. I don't find that to be a threat. Anytime we are invited to take a new view of something of which we think we have all the necessary knowledge, and are forced to get out of our comfort zone in order to take a hard look at and to examine what it is we really think about something, big or small, we resist. Much of (most of) religion has little to do with faith. Religion is an attempt to answer as many questions as possible in terms we can understand as humans about a Deity that we cannot possibly understand this side of eternity. I don't mean to imply that religion is a bad thing, but it is a function of faith, not the other way around. Faith can be expressed by religion up to a point, but religion is just that—an expression. It is a means of finding a community of fellow believers expressing a faith that is similar enough that they can all find comfort worshipping together. It is not God in and of itself, but rather a human institution, influenced by God, but ultimately controlled by and subject to the agendas of men. The simple fact that there are as many denominations of Christianity as there are proves the "humanness" of religion. If God had created religion without the influence of man after the fact, wouldn't there be a single Christian denomination? I'll not get into the non-Christian believers in the world, because I haven't enough knowledge to do so. But for us to believe that our own brand of Christianity is the only true one, and that those who worship elsewhere are somehow inferior, or unworthy of God's love and forgiveness, presumes to know more about the Mind of God than we truly can. As for this book, it merely points to our humanity and the shortcomings therein, and invites the reader to offer room for a different point of view. It does not say that by living just so we can eliminate evil from human behavior. On the contrary. It only shows that how we behave now is not as Creation was originally intended and that ultimately, in spite of that fact, the omnipotence of God will prevail. No more, no less.

14

Ministry

During my life I have had contact with a number of men of the cloth from various denominations, primarily Catholic and Lutheran. Most of these men have been good men, interested in the spiritual well-being of the people in their charge. Some have been self-serving, political, greedy and not at all interested in the business of the vocation that should have called them to the ministry. During the past ten years or so the scandal of the sexual abuse of young people by priests has been a struggle for those Catholics who were raised to believe that the men of the priesthood were above reproach. They were seen as examples of how men and woman should comport themselves on this earth, in this life. When the stories emerged about the damage they had done to the people in their charge, the young people, helpless and naive, afraid and trusting young people, the stories did damage to the faithful that may never be undone. The disbelief that accompanied the stories of these men's sins remained for some, even in the face of the final acknowledgement by the Church that the actions really did take place and that the Church had covered it up. It has been my misfortune to have had experience with men of the cloth, both priests and bishops, who, for reasons known only to them, behaved in ways that disillusioned their followers and drove them from the Church. In the case of the Catholic Church, much of this disillusionment has to do with the hierarchy of the body, the lack of accountability to the people in the pews for any actions they take. It has to do with the fact that, although they encourage parishioners to take roles on various boards and committees, the final word, no matter what the majority may agree to, belongs to the priest and the bishop. When everyone is in agreement, the illusion of parish contributions to the decision-making process remains intact. But if there is disagreement, and if the priest chooses to exercise the authority given him by the hierarchy, that illusion is destroyed.

I have seen the same kind of thing happen in other denominations, where the pastor manipulates the faithful in such a way so as to have things go exactly as he wishes. Rarely does he get challenged, but when he does, his knowledge of how the game is played has allowed him to already have put people into positions of authority in the congregation who will support him, or at the very least not challenge his authority. He can also count on the hierarchy of the Church to support him, because to not is to undermine the authority they themselves hold over the faithful. Recently a challenge to the current pastor's authority has created a drama where the people express their disapproval of their pastor, the pastor responds with threats of excommunication, a representative of the district becomes involved, and the real possibility of a split in the congregation emerges. For people together trying to find God, this is a tragedy. It only shows how personally one's faith is embedded and how we respond when our faith is challenged by what we perceive to be a threat to that faith.

Men who have chosen the ministry as a career have done so for a variety of reasons, some noble, some not so. Some young men are truly called by God to serve His Church. Some respond to the challenge, some do not. As young men who have been perhaps a little out of place in school for whatever reason, the ministry offers some rather attractive incentives. First, and perhaps most laudable, these men may have developed a faith more mature than their popular peers. Some just hear the call to the vocation and respond. Some, by not being recognized for their accomplishments in sports or other more popular aspects of a teen's identity, have perhaps spent more introspective time studying who they are, who they want to be in life. As idealistic young men they may arrive at the conclusion that they were meant to be ministers, and that the lack of esteem given them as young men set them apart for just such a vocation. These are the ones who should be ministers. They offer the potential to lead good lives, to inspire others by their example and to lead a congregation to better communion with God.

However, not all instincts are quite so noble. It is apparent to most that when one puts on a collar, he receives automatic respect and trust from total strangers when he arrives at a new assignment. Only if he gives his parishioners reason to distrust him or lose respect for him does that initial automatic reaction disappear. For someone who has never had that kind of respect, this is a tempting career to choose, regardless of whether he has the potential to become a good pastor. Another temptation, at least in the Catholic Church, is the fact that there is no need to explain not having a family. Celibacy is a mandate for the priesthood, so not having a wife is nothing to have to justify. If a man's sexual identity leads him towards homosexuality or pedophilia, the priesthood provides an opportunity to hide in plain sight. This does not automatically disqualify a man from the ministry, but if the temptation to act upon his sexual tendencies becomes insurmountable, he puts himself in a position to at least be a scandal to the world. At worst, if those inclinations lead him to prey upon the defenseless in his care, it becomes much worse than scandal. In the fifties and sixties, when most of the men who would later be involved in the Church's scandal were choosing a career, practicing overt homosexuality was not an option in a society that considered it an unnatural lifestyle and made no excuses for it's condemnation. As a result men who wanted the respect of their peers without judgment for their proclivities may have chosen the priesthood.

In any event, for whatever reason a man becomes a minister, the responsibilities and temptations implicit in the ministry should give him pause. Many men, men whom I've known personally, have fit into the category of good men, capable of inspiring goodness in others and capable of withstanding whatever personal temptations they may face. Unfortunately, I have also come to know men who have no business in the ministry, no potential to shepherd God's people. I have met those who, if they ever attained ordination, probably did do damage to the young people in their charge. I have met those who have used their vocations for self-aggrandizement and financial benefit for themselves and their families, and simply to hold a position that allowed themselves to feel worthy in their own small world. Sometimes a man can be inspirational and selfish at the same time, but sooner or later these two aspects of that personality will collide, and anger will result. If a minister without the real vocation is challenged by someone in his charge, his anger may be the result of that lack of respect he experienced as a young man. As an adult, that anger may seem completely disproportionate to the perceived insult. The anger may be a symptom of one trying to attain a goal that is always just out of reach—the respect he has always felt he deserved but never received.

The ministry in any denomination should be a sacred calling. To presume that it is anything less does a disservice to the vocation and to those men who have served that vocation with honor. My church in particular is continuing to try to atone for the abuses of its ministers, and my wife's church is in the middle of a different kind of abuse of power right now. As long as men whose intentions are less than honorable continue to pursue careers in the ministry this kind of thing will go on. As long as there is a shortage of ministers, the men in charge of winnowing out the men who will do no service to the church will be tempted to overlook the warning signs. As long as the hierarchy of the church remains as it is, the same kinds of abuses will continue. In my church married men may not pursue a vocation to the priesthood, nor can women. Many will say that it's that way because it's always been that way and it shouldn't be changed. Tradition is all-important. But it hasn't always been that way. In the beginning of the Church the leaders of the faithful, the apostles and those that followed in their footsteps as priests and bishops, were married men with families. It wasn't until the Church decided that there may be a financial price the Church may have to pay to support these families that the tradition of a celibate, unmarried priesthood evolved. Maybe that was a just decision at the time, maybe not. But right now I don't believe that an unmarried, celibate priesthood serves any good purpose. I think a better group of candidates would be attracted to the ministry without those prerequisites. A healthier, more centered man (or woman), having gifts to offer, unhindered by the demons that currently lurk in the shadows of the personalities of some of the men in the ministry today, would step up and take their rightful place among those whose vocation it is to lead souls to Heaven. The hiding place for homosexuals and pedophiles would no longer be there. When the scandals of the priesthood began forty-plus years ago, these men were looked upon as unworthy in society. The men who fit in that category found comfort in a profession that not only allowed an unmarried man but demanded it. As a result they found themselves in a position of respect and trust that gave them access to defenseless young boys with little or no supervision because they already had the trust of the parents of those boys. If a complaint was lodged, the bishops just moved them to another parish and the cycle started all over again. If heterosexual men were allowed into the priesthood and allowed to marry and have families the threat of this kind of abuse would be greatly minimized, and men with great gifts as ministers would be allowed to share those gifts with parishes who now have no one. A new tradition would be born, based on the original tradition of the Church for its ministry, capable of raising the vocation of priest to a position deserving of its honor and respect—and trust.

As in any other political forum, though, the ones with the power to effect change in an institution are the ones who would be affected most by those changes. Our legislative branch of government won't pass laws to limit the time spent in office because the legislators would be the ones put out of work, thus lessening the power and prestige they desire. In the same way, churches could make changes to the the way they call ministers and to make those ministers accountable to the people they were called to serve. But this, too, would lessen the things many of the ones who have no business in the ministry crave—power, prestige, respect and trust. I don't anticipate that these changes will occur in my lifetime. If there's one thing I've learned over the years in observing the workings of established institutions it is that change occurs with glacial speed. So I'll just write about my frustrations and the frustrations I've witnessed in others like me. If Vatican III ever happens, I'd like to be a witness to the changes that may come about in it's wake. Until that happens, we'll see . . . .

15

The Institutional Church

There was an announcement on the radio this morning concerning the "rehabilitation" by Pope Gregory XVI of four bishops who had been excommunicated by Pope John Paul II back in 1984. These men were (and are) members of an organization called the Society of St. Pius X, one of whom had denied the holocaust. The Society of St Pius X was founded in the early 1970's by French Archbishop Marcel Lefebvre, himself excommunicated, as a reaction to the Second Vatican Council, calling for a return to the Tridentine Mass, a dissolution of any Catholic body involved in trying to reach unity among Christian denominations and a cessation of any dialogue between Catholics and Jews. The organization was not recognized by the Vatican because its actions betrayed a failure to recognize papal supremacy, among other things. Whether or not one agrees with the reasons for the original excommunications or the failure to recognize the organization, the recent action to rescind the excommunications with no apologies or changes in attitude by the four bishops points to the subjectivity of decisions made by the hierarchy of the Church. First of all, why would the Church find it desirable to reinstate them, and second, why would the individuals involved want to be reinstated? I have no problem with reinstating a member of the Church if the attitudes that led to the excommunication have changed and the individual has proven to have contrition for those attitudes. But to reinstate them as bishops, and with no remorse or change in attitude by them proves that there is no real standard by which they are judged. So what standard do we apply to the actions of the Church itself? And ultimately, what standard do we apply to ourselves? It has been said that if one accepts the teachings of any individual regarding faith, whether that be a pope, Martin Luther, John Calvin, the Dalai Lama or anyone else, without a mature examination of what one believes about one's own faith, means that one must take responsibility for any errors in those teachings as well as for the truths contained therein. Do we, as Catholics or any other denomination, abide by the instructions of another, or must we decide for ourselves what code to live by?

Thus my dilemma. Thus my problem with the institutional Catholic Church. Thus my decision to remain a cafeteria Catholic.

16

Conflict

I am in conflict. I would like to go to Confession, but some of the things the Church believes to be sinful I do not. If I go to Confession and knowingly do not confess the things that I have done or have not done that the Church would find fault with, then as I was taught as a child about confession, I would not be forgiven for anything. And if I confess to things that I personally do not feel are sinful, I am not being true to my own sense of morality. If I do not attend Mass on Sundays or Holy Days, do not abstain from eating meat on Fridays during Lent, do not agree with or abide by the Church's teachings on birth control, do not adhere to the Church's rule of going to Confession at least once a year, do not acknowledge the authority of the men in the Church's hierarchy in the institutional Church in all things related to religion, do not contribute monetarily to the Church out of principle or if I do or do not do something else in conflict with the Church's teachings, am I then obliged to confess these things whether or not I believe in their validity? If I confide to a priest outside the confessional of my conflict and he disagrees with my position, is he obliged to deny me the sacraments until and unless I agree to the conditions of the Church? Attendance at Mass, reception of Holy Communion, proclaiming the readings—all these things come into risk if I broach the subject with a man of the cloth. I have been away from the Church for periods of time during my life and I would like not to leave again, but there are aspects of my personal adult faith that conflict with what I was taught in catechism as a child. I am aware of the Church's teaching about forgiveness through an act of perfect contrition when facing death in the absence of a priest, but at what point does an act of contrition become "perfect", and when is it an exercise in futility if confession is not part of the process when it is available?

I was raised as a Catholic, and I feel that the faith I practice is Catholic to the extent that I follow my personal moral compass and do not conflict with the basic moral principles taught by the Church. Much of what I disagree with has to do with decisions made by the men in the hierarchy, which, throughout history, have been proven to be subject to revision by future leaders. In my adult life experiences I have determined that not all morality comes from Rome, and there are certain areas of what I believe that may be more in line with different religious disciplines. So at what point do I surrender my own faith to something or someone that I don't believe represents my own morality? Isn't that a form of heresy in and of itself? The basis for a good confession is a thorough examination of conscience. If my conscience does not see sin in non-conformity to some of the requirements of the Church then what is the point of the exercise?

So, I am in conflict. It will require some prayer and probably a great risk to what it is that I hold dear to make a decision in the matter. I believe that as long as I am true to myself and my personal morality, which includes most of the precepts of the Church, I will meet God in Heaven when I die. But confession is still good for the soul, and I'd like to go again.

17

Eternal Family

When we reach Heaven will we be greeted by other souls who have been here on earth and arrived before us? Will we know only those whom we have known here on earth, or will we know everyone? Will we even care about any others but God when we reach there? We have been told of meeting parents and grandparents and friends when we arrive, but we have been told that by ones who have never been there, who are trying to give us comfort in our grief by telling us of things we may encounter that are familiar to us. We have heard stories of those who, in the immediacy of a near-death experience have seen loved ones who have passed on ahead, seen a bright light and other phenomena. These may be a real prelude of what we may experience in death. But these experiences may also be the result of chemical changes in our body's adjustment to stress, such as adrenaline or epinephrine, nothing more. Our experience in Heaven may be just as people have described it, happily being reunited with friends and family and experiencing Divine love. It may also be that we will be so entranced by the experience of being with the Almighty that we won't even notice the presence of others, familiar or not. Our existence in the hereafter will likely have little to do with anything we have experienced in the here and now, so any prediction of such an existence is without proof. Simply the presence of God may be all that consumes our eternal existence and experience, and being in the presence of family and friends and saints and angels may be of little or no consequence.

18

Demons In the World

It's always puzzled me—In the Bible, especially in the New Testament, there are references made to the casting out of demons by Jesus and his followers. Not so much these days. Few discount the presence of demons in our world today, but accounts of them are rare. Does this mean that there were more demons present in the world at that time; that "demons" were actually illnesses, such as epilepsy or schizophrenia, that we now recognize and treat as illness; that Jesus' birth, death and resurrection restricted the powers of demons over humans; or were they opportunities for showing the power of Jesus as the Son of God? Or was it something else entirely?

19

Gospels

There are four gospels, Matthew, Mark, Luke and John, the first three called the "synoptic gospels" and John. There are notable similarities as well as dissimilarities in each. There have been debates since the beginning as to when each was written, who copied from whom, whether they were indeed written by the individuals to whom credit has been given and why the differences. Mark is the shortest and has been said to have been both influence of and influenced by the other two synoptic gospels. There has been debate over whether the Gospel of John was written by the same "John" as wrote the three Letters of John and the Book of Revelation, not to mention whether the letters and Revelation were written by the same man. The gospels were anonymous until about 180 AD when suddenly they were ascribed to the four evangelists. None were probably written until at least 50 years after the life of Christ. Is this a problem?

First of all, events witnessed by humans are invariably seen, remembered and interpreted differently by as many witnesses as there are to an event. This is not uncommon. Second, if indeed the gospels were written so many years after the death of Jesus, would there not be some unconscious editing done by the authors simply by virtue if the time passed? And finally, if these authors were inspired to write the Word of God, as we believe them to have been, and if the gospels were each written to a different audience, wouldn't the treatment of the material vary a bit based on that audience as well as on the style of the authors?

Read side by side, the gospels differ by either the inclusion or exclusion of some details of the Life of Christ. None are duplicates of the others, or why go to the effort? But the inclusion of some details and the exclusion of others tell us different things about the God/Man we claim belief in. Some include details of his nativity, some more about his human lineage, and in the case of Mark don't mention his birth or young life at all until his baptism in the Jordan by the baptist. Some speak of different miracles, parables, friends and enemies. Some describe the Last Supper in different ways and on different days. Some describe differences in their description of the events of Good Friday, from Gethsemane to His death on the cross. There are differences regarding who went to the tomb on Easter morning, who awaited them, how, when and where Jesus appeared to his disciples after the Resurrection. But I find the differences not so much a problem as a fuller, richer depiction of the thirty years Jesus spent here on earth. They also give a difference as to how we see this Man, Jesus. He is the Christ, he is the Word, he is the Lamb of God, he is the fulfillment of scripture, he is God. All these things give us peace and confidence, even if they are not all written in every account of His life.

There is a reason why there is a different evangelist given priority in each liturgical year. We get a different way of seeing the life of Christ than the year before and the year after. We get more details about how he lived, who he encountered, the acts he performed, the messages he taught. And we get all these things in a more coherent way than if all the gospels were scattered throughout the liturgical year, with no rhyme or sequence to them except that each gospel reading might have something to do with the particular week's events. During this year Mark's is the dominant gospel, but being as short as it is, and excluding as much of the feasts we celebrate as it does, we are required to add others to the mix. But in those years when the gospel narrative includes accounts of most or all of the celebrations we have, such as last year's emphasis on Matthew's gospel, we hear one man's view of the life of Christ, with all the details he deems important to the narrative and the absence of those he does not. Even those missing cause us to think for ourselves about those missing stories, why they are missing and why we find them important. This is an important aspect of a self-examination of our faith.

20

Anger

Is being angry with God about death a sin or just being human? If you believe in the Garden of Eden story, being human is being sinful, so is being angry with God a sin? If you have a loved one in pain or dying, if you're going through a bitter divorce, getting fired from your job or just losing the big game, depending on where your priorities are, is it morally wrong to assign blame to the One who has all the power and to be angry with Him about it? There is one unavoidable given about being human—we will none of us get out of this alive. Someday, under circumstances of which we are as yet probably unaware, we will die. It's inevitable, we can't change that. So when it happens, whenever it happens and under whatever circumstances it happens, do we have the right to question the time and the means and the circumstances of that inevitability? We all do to some extent, whether we wish to admit it or not, but is it something to be ashamed of or can we justify the anger? My wife's grandmother, who lived to be 104 and buried her husband and some of her children wondered out loud why God let her live and took the lives of her children, and I've never met a more saintly woman than she was. I saw my sister die a painful death at the age of 21, and saw the same question in my mother's face for the next 30 years. My daughter-in-law's mother is dying of cancer, and in great pain and in great anger I see it, I see the same questioning and blame in her face—"Why me? Why her? Why now? Why so much pain? Why?", and the anger at the only One with the power to change it. But is it wrong to have those feelings, to lash out at God in prayer or in lack thereof, to have your faith challenged or even diminished as a result? Is it even something we can control? I've heard all the pious arguments from people in the business of God, explaining

Him and His actions, excusing them, justifying them, encouraging you to have faith and accept His will without question. It doesn't usually work, at least not in the short term. After it's over and you've come to accept the inevitability of death and are no longer affected by the pain and suffering involved, maybe your faith is restored. But is it ever the same? And was it sinful at the time to be angry about it? I don't think so.

We are who we are, humans with human frailties. Yes, there are saints among us, but we find if we look that even those saintly people had their doubts and questions. I think this, too, is inevitable. Can we be truly faithful without asking questions about what it is we are supposed to have faith in? Can we aspire to live a faith-filled life if we haven't taken the time and energy to examine those parts of our faith that give us pause in times of crisis? If we haven't tried to discover for ourselves what it is we have faith in, what our faith is and what the truth is, our basis for faith, then how can we be faithful? Some think that questions mean a lack of faith, but I don't think faith is possible without questions. Some teach of a child-like faith, and how ideal that is. To see that kind of faith in a child is to be expected, but should we expect it in a mature adult? Have all the philosophers and theologians down through history not studied their philosophies and theologies without questioning what it was they were trying to get a handle on, what they were trying to get across to their students? There are some things in life that we cannot comprehend with our limited abilities, but does that mean we are not allowed to be angry at our incomprehension, or that that anger is sinful in and of itself? No. We are who we are. We are not demi-gods, we are not powerful to the extent that we are able to change the unchangeable. Doctors can at times delay the inevitable, but they cannot preclude its inevitability. We were created in love, and unless we are somehow psychologically damaged, we love. We have to love someone, something, somehow. To not get angry at the pain and imminent death of someone we love is to deny who we are and what we were created for. Therefore, is it a sin to be angry, even at God, at times like this? I don't think so. Anger may not be required, but it is not forbidden, either. We are who we are. Along with the love with which we were created are other passions, including anger and frustration and pity and a need to try to protect those we love. We even have sorrow and pain for the loss of some we don't know, if the circumstances of their deaths are tragic. Doesn't that make us human? Isn't that who we were created to be? Doesn't that make our anger, even at God, acceptable behavior, as long as that anger doesn't drive us from Him? Anger, too, is what we were created for. God Himself has shown anger under certain circumstances, and we are created in His image. So under some circumstances, anger is acceptable, not sinful, not unfaithful, not unjustified, just human. Our time here on earth is to try to be more God-like, but to think we can be less human is foolish. We are who we are. We are who we were created to be. To be more than that we'll have to wait until Heaven, and have faith that there and then we will be who were were ultimately intended to be. Until then if we are angry, it's okay. Just have faith that the anger will pass, and in the opinion of those men and women of God, the crises that caused the anger will in fact make our faith stronger. This, too, I believe is true. But getting past the anger takes time, more for some than for others. Most of the time it doesn't drive us away from God, but it probably does fundamentally change our faith in Him, hopefully for the better. But in any event we are who we were created to be.

21

Religion & Relationships

Recently I heard a coworker decry Catholics as "Idol-Worshipers." It angered me deeply and immediately. I have heard others dismiss Catholicism vis-a-vis Lutheranism because of Mary and our practice of praying to saints as if it were worship or adoration. I have tried to explain that we do not pray to saints for actions or miracles, but when some do it is rather for intercession, asking that they pray to God on our behalf, and we don't all do even that. The response is that as a Lutheran they don't believe in intermediaries, but rather pray to God directly. I expect they speak for most protestants from an education about Catholicism, what justification existed for a break with the Catholic Church back when and how it differs from their own religion. These lessons were learned as a young person and carry over into adulthood. I personally don't see why the difference would, in and of itself, create an insurmountable division between two groups of Catholic-Christians to the point that a different denomination of Christianity was born. I understand that there were other factors that entered into the Protestant Reformation, many of them justifiable. I also know that most of those factors had been resolved long before I was born. I also know that my religion is not perfect as an institution, but neither is any other.

In my catechism years as a child, and during my studies at St. John's as a young man, I don't recall many discussions regarding the differences between my religion and others. I don't know if that was because we felt that the other denominations were latecomers and as such didn't merit a comparison with the Catholic faith. Ours was, after all, the first Christian faith and therefore the only true faith. We maybe didn't feel the need to justify our existence as perhaps other later denominations did. Protestantism, Judaism, Islam and any other "non-Catholic" entities were just not worth the discussion. But that was in an earlier time in history. I believe that Catholicism has progressed beyond that and now respects the beliefs of other faiths and their right to express those beliefs in worship. I think that those other "non-Catholic" religions are respected for what they are—a means to try to find God and to reach Heaven, different but worthy of respect, nevertheless. I would hope that the same respect is offered my church as well.

22

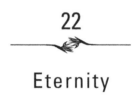

Eternity

Time is a very human necessity. We use minutes and hours and days and nights to determine when we work and play and sleep. We use months and years to measure our progress through life, from birth to death. Spring, summer, autumn and winter help us to time when we plant and harvest and let the earth rest and renew itself. Time is of this world.

In Genesis we find a description of how the earth was created. It took God six days to do His work, and then He rested. He didn't need the rest, but rather gave us an example so that part of each week we would rest and renew ourselves. Time is of this world.

Eternity has no time element. There is no beginning and no end. Rather it is a state of being. This past week I sat at my mother's bedside watching her die. Twenty years ago I watched my father die, and thirty years ago, my sister. And so it goes, back to the beginning of time. I believe that when we die we arrive at an eternity without time. I believe that all who have gone before and all who will follow arrive at that same eternity at the same time. Parents and children, ancestors and descendants, no matter when we lived on earth, we will all arrive at the same eternity at once. I believe that we are guided through our time here on earth by all those who have preceded us and all who will come later. I believe that my time here on earth has been influenced by those who have loved me in eternity, whether they be ancestors or descendants, and that at those moments when I find myself faced with a moral choice, someone in eternity tries to influence that decision toward the good. We grieve here on earth for those we have loved who have gone, but that grieving is temporal. Those who have gone do not have to wait for us to follow, because we are there already.

23

Other Gods

It has been puzzling to me for a long time to see God's acknowledgment of "other gods" in Scripture. Even in the Ten Commandments from Sinai, "I am the Lord, your God. You shall not have strange gods before me." Joshua made reference to the gods from beyond the river, and the gods of the Amorites, before he stated that, "As for me and my house, we will serve the Lord." I know that men of all civilizations have served gods from the beginning, but if there is only one God, why even acknowledge the possibility of other gods. Is this merely a means of communicating with man in terms he can understand, with foreknowledge of man's predisposition to worship false gods? Why not simply deny the existence of any other gods, to say that I am the only God, not that thou shall not have other gods, but that there are no other gods? I'm sure there is reason for God's reference to other gods, and for His prophets to do the same, I just don't understand its justification.

24

Lector

It has been my privilege and honor to proclaim the Word to the congregation during mass. It has been my goal to discover the meaning of the text and to relay it in such a way that it seems real to the listeners. I have tried to find a way to speak in such a manner as I would should I be talking to them in normal conversation, using the same inflections, pauses, emphasis and expression as I would use in everyday communication, though with the respect and dignity the text deserves. Given the ancient use of language and some of the words and phrases and the context in which they are used, this can be a challenge. But I try my best. I don't know how it comes across to all of the people, but I have had enough encouragement and expressions of appreciation from some that I think I may be on the right track. As a result, I think my responsibility is to make the readings from the Old and the New Testaments to be real and understandable to the congregation, rather than just be able to speak the words without losing my place, mispronunciation, in something other than a monotone, trying not to put people to sleep. Some efforts are more successful than others, I know, because of the difficulty of the readings or because of my own inability to express the intent of the text coherently. But when I do it right, I know it, and it feels good. It feels as if I have contributed to a liturgy with more meaning than it might otherwise have for those in the pews. I know from personal experience that when you have said the same prayers and given the same responses to prayers during the liturgy for as many years as most of us have, it becomes more of a rote exercise, and the meaning, though understandable, is not appreciated. We speak the words without thinking about what we're saying. One gets to the end of the service and wonder what just happened and where did the hour go. I see my role as lector as one who brings life to the liturgy, and tries to make modern sense out of ancient texts, so that the meaning of the words is appreciated rather than merely heard. If people hear a message that they might otherwise miss, then I have done my job.

25

Poetry

There's a friend of mine who writes poetry and likes to have me read it. The poetry is good stuff as far as I know, but it follows a pretty consistent theme. It deals primarily with man's moral failures, condemnation for those failures and the forgiveness brought by Jesus' death and resurrection. This isn't a bad theme, but from the poetry he brings to me, the topic is much on his mind. I'm trying to decide whether the obsession with man's failure is a healthy thing. Yes, I believe that the Savior having come into the world is indeed a comforting reality, and all his writings end with that reality. But it makes me wonder about the state of his emotional health if most of each poem deals with that failure as the only thing about which he finds worthy of writing. He has a fundamental religious bent to all his thoughts and, yes, judgments about life and mankind here on earth. It reminds me of the strict interpretations of religion I was taught as a child from the Baltimore Catechism, an unapologetically conservative and judgmental doctrine espoused by the Roman Catholic church of the fifties and before. He did attend Catholic schools as a young man, and considered himself Catholic at one time, but not anymore. His membership in the Evangelical Free church now comes, I believe, with a teaching that we are saved. And yet his obsession with man's failure and sinfulness and the real possibility of eternal damnation leads me to believe that he's not sure if he's on God's naughty or nice list. His conclusions about eternal salvation seem to imply a confidence that the possibility exists, but much of the poetry also implies a worry about his own, maybe mankind's, expectation of that salvation. Yes, we are by nature sinful beings, and yes we will remain so in spite of our best efforts to change our behavior. And yet we are assured of salvation through Jesus, in spite of those shortcomings. But at what point in our consideration of these realities does the realization of our sinfulness become harmful to our outlook on life and how we live and enjoy the graces we've been given? Does an obsession with the former destroy the latter? His attitudes in general are somewhat rigid, conservative and judgmental. Is this just his personality or did his religious epiphanies during a lifetime of sinfulness create that personality? Was he attracted to the religious leanings he now holds as a result of a personality looking for a comfortable fit, or was it the other way around? Is the poetry he writes simply a means of putting down on paper a confidence in salvation, or is it a depiction of a personality burdened with a premonition that, if he hasn't led a good enough life or had enough faith in salvation, that eternal damnation is imminent? In either event, if that's the way the Old Testament prophets told their stories, it's no wonder they were all killed.

We both know that we have different outlooks on life, politics and, to some extent, religion. He is more conservative, I more liberal. I look at life with some comfort in the knowledge that, in spite of a lifetime of sinfulness, I need not be troubled about eternity. I have become comfortable with my faith and who I am. The forgiveness written at the end of his poetry would, in my case, take up most of my own writings, not just the last stanza. I look at my existence here on earth as a blessing—a gift from God to revel in and to be happy about. I have known family and friends who have given me great comfort. I have raised a family and seen the product of that enterprise as truly miraculous, watching as the young ones grow and learn and reflect the values and behaviors of probably many more generations than I am even aware, passed down over millennia from the beginning. My faith is a confidence that I will see God. His seems more uncertain, and his views of existence here on earth are more about the turmoils of being human and the weaknesses inherent therein. His a more Old Testament faith with the salvation story added in. He sees not as much joy in living as he might, and that, I guess, is the point of this. I feel sorry for him, but I'm not certain if I should. I wish him peace—peace on earth, here, now, not just a hopeful eternity someday.

26

Salvation or Damnation?

This is not intended to be an apology for Satan. Satan and his legions were damned for their rebellion against God. They are, nevertheless, creations of God, as are the good angels and as are we. Therefore, they were created in the image and likeness of God. We have all rebelled against the Father, but based on our faith, we are forgiven, if only we choose to accept His grace. We are promised eternal salvation based on the sacrifice of His Son. Now, I understand that damnation is eternal, both for Satan and for those humans who choose not to avail themselves of Christ's offer of salvation. But in what way are we like Satan insofar as we are all creations of the Father? To what degree are we able to merit salvation, even if that only comes at the end of life? I've been taught that living as rightly as we can during our time here on earth makes that salvation more likely, and that living wrongly makes it more difficult to atone for the sins of a lifetime at the end, even if we have the time to make that decision. During the course of eternal damnation or eternal salvation, are we or the devil ever able to change our minds regarding our eternal reward, either good or bad? Do any of those souls in heaven ever feel the temptation to rebel as Satan did, regardless of their current state of salvation? Are any of the souls in hell able to surrender their wills to God and hope for salvation? What makes that decision irrevocable, either here on earth or in eternity? If we were all created with free will, as I believe we were, at what point does that free will stop giving us, damned or saved, here or in eternity, the ability to become something other than what we are at the moment?

I'm not trying to say that Satan will change. I'm not saying that either eternal damnation or eternal salvation are less than eternal. My question is, does Satan decide, at the moment of our death, that that particular battle for the soul is over? Does the end of the world and the second coming signal the end of the battle between God and Satan, between Good and Evil? Satan sinned in eternity, during an existence of heavenly rapture. Does that mean that we could sin in eternity as well, whether or not we have been saved? Or do we no longer have the ability to rebel, as we have here on earth and as Satan did in Heaven? And if not, why not? If not, what happened to free will? Will our experience in Heaven be fundamentally different than Satan's was?

As I said, this was not intended to be a defense of Satan. This is only an examination of what has come before and what we have to look forward to in eternity. I do not necessarily challenge the teachings of the Church or the Gospels as we have been given them. I believe what Jesus said regarding salvation. I only wonder about the difference between rebellion in eternity before Eden and the lack of rebellion in eternity after.

27

The Salvation Story

I am a Catholic Christian and this is not intended to question the teachings of my Church or any other Christian denomination. I do not question the veracity of the teachings regarding the nativity, the life, death, resurrection and ascension of the salvation story. That is not what this is about.

God created man. He placed him in the garden of Eden, the closest thing to paradise this side of Heaven. He allowed him to sin and then banished him from Eden. The Old Testament speaks to the suffering, the sinfulness of man, and the anticipation of a Savior from God. My question is not whether that is true, but whether it was necessary. I know that we were created with free will and we, from Adam on down, sinned against God. I know that God desired reconciliation between Himself and those He created. I know that Jesus was sent to accomplish that reconciliation, became man, lived, suffered, died and rose, thus accomplishing the salvation story. We are now free to take advantage of that salvation act or not. But why go to all that trouble? He spoke through the prophets to make Himself and His wishes for mankind known, so why not just decide, "I wish to forgive a sinful creation, so, THEY ARE FORGIVEN." Forget about the entire act of sending His Son to earth to accomplish something that He could have done as easily as He created man in the first place. Simply send another prophet 2000 years ago (or whenever) to tell His people that they are stupid, but they are forgiven. Period. The Jews listened to and believed that the prophets of old spoke for God, so why not another prophet, speaking for Him and proclaiming forgiveness for man's stubbornness and sinfulness? Was it necessary to accomplish the salvation of mankind through the suffering and death of God's Son in order to reconcile God with man? Was it necessary to make Him like one of us in all things but sin? Could He have not just remained seated at the right hand of the Father and not spent 30 years down here?

An entire religion has been created as a result of the life of Jesus on this earth, and as a result most of our belief surrounding Heaven and hell, salvation and damnation has become the religion of a great many of the world's populace over millennia. This in spite of the fact that the Jews were originally intended to be His people. Why not still? I know that many would have killed the prophet that was sent to proclaim forgiveness, just as many of their predecessors were. But many would have accepted salvation gratefully, just as the Christians have. So again, why go to the trouble of sending a Savior?

I suppose this goes to the same question many of us ask when troubles arise in our lives, death and illness, pain and suffering: "Why me? Why now? Why?" As Christians we are told to have faith that God has a plan, and whether we know it or not, there is a reason for what happens to us here on earth, both good and bad. We simply don't know God's plan. So it stands to reason that the same questions may arise regarding the Christ coming to earth as the only means of salvation for mankind. He did. But why?

28

Personal Integrity

"Stress may be more a matter of personal integrity than time pressure, determined by the difference between our authentic values and how we live our lives." Rachel Naomi Remen, M.D., from "My Grandfather's Blessings."

Finding one's own personal integrity is a lifelong search. When we think we have discovered integrity we find another layer hidden beneath, much like an onion. We all find ourselves under stress in our lives, whether we be children trying to please, to fit in or to excel, or a teenager trying to find the strength to discover who we are and attempting to not follow someone else's idea of who it is we should be. It may be as a young parent or a new employee, trying to seem like we know what we are doing and getting the respect we desire from a spouse, a parent, a coworker or a boss, regardless of how unprepared we may feel to perform the job required. It may be as a member of the community, a business person, a committee member, a peer among those with whom we'd like to be associated and admired. Time is always a factor in our lives and takes much of the blame for those things we can't seem to get accomplished, or for those things that we fail at, thus causing stress. But if we look closely at what it is that really causes us to stress, we may come face to face with the reality of the dichotomy between what it is we believe, what our core values are, and how we behave. We know right from wrong as we believe it to be, but we may have skewed that knowledge in order to create a persona that is someone other than who we really are.

Personal integrity is something very personal between us and God. It may not be the same personal integrity that our neighbor recognizes, and in fact probably couldn't be. Each of us has evolved from our own personal set of circumstances and life experiences, and as a result our integrity is uniquely our own. It is not the same as the formal integrity we may find by following the Ten Commandments, for example, but rather it means being true to who it is that we are, honestly, and with no superficial dressing to hide that being. When we find that real, honest integrity and the peace that accompanies it, we relax a bit and find that stress is less a factor in our lives. But we also find another layer that needs to be explored if we are to find our ultimate personal integrity. This may never come to a full realization, or if it does, it may not happen until death. That's okay, though, as long as we continue to explore the layers beneath. With each layer exposed we become more honest with ourselves and less stressful.

Integrity comes from the word integral, or essential, fundamental. To become aware of what our own personal integrity entails is necessary to finding peace—peace with ourselves and peace with God. Encountering that fundamental essence of who we are allows us to remove much of the stress of living that we generally blame on something else. It allows us to become self-aware, secure in the knowledge that our own personal integrity has been recognized and accepted for what it is, for who we are—really, honestly, and to live our lives in such a way as to enjoy peace and harmony with others and with ourselves. What a stress reliever that is!

29

Eucharist

Mine is a eucharistic religion. When we gather to celebrate the Mass it is with the sole purpose of celebrating and commemorating the Eucharist instituted at the Last Supper. The central theme of our liturgy is the sacrament, and everything leads up to that climax. We have the readings from the Old Testament and the Epistle as well the Gospel reading for the day, a homily, the Creed and all the other parts of the Mass, but the Consecration and distribution of the Eucharist is what it's all about.

I have talked to members of other denominations and attended other non-Catholic services. My wife's Lutheran service has the Eucharistic liturgy about twice a month. The rest of the Sunday worship services are Matins or Vespers, with the readings and the homily as the primary focus of the liturgy. The other Lutheran denomination here in town has a celebration of the Eucharist, but they don't believe that the Body and the Blood are really present in the bread and wine. Other denominations deal primarily with the Word of God with little attention paid to the Eucharist at all as instituted on Maundy Thursday. They believe that the Word is what it's all about, and reading it and teaching about it is more important than the the Eucharist. They look down on Catholic liturgy because they believe it doesn't give enough import to Scripture.

In searching for God it is my opinion that when Jesus said, "Do this in memory of me . . ." he had a reason. I agree that perhaps not enough attention is paid to the Word during the Mass, but there are other means of giving attention to the Scripture if we only make the effort to find it—Bible studies, private reading, liturgy of hours, perpetual adoration and others. But as far as the celebration of Mass is concerned, Eucharist is what it is.

30

Sacramental Grace

There is a certain grace that comes from the reception of a sacrament. I recently read someone who said that that grace is already affecting our life as we prepare ourselves for the sacrament, incrementally from the moment the decision to receive the sacrament is made. I hadn't thought about it in that way before, but it is true. Part of the grace allows us to make the decision in the first place, and continues to influence our preparations for that sacrament right up to and beyond the reception.

If the sacrament we approach is confirmation, marriage, ordination or whatever, it takes grace to decide for ourselves to approach it in the first place. It takes grace to prepare for the sacrament and to carry out the responsibilities of that sacrament once received. The grace is not poured out on us only at the moment of the reception, but in fact is received throughout the period leading up to the sacrament. It is also that grace that gives us the authority to live up to the sacrament after reception.

31

Fishermen

There is an account in Luke's gospel about Peter, James and John, all fishermen by trade, being called to follow Jesus. Jesus had just told them to put out into the deep waters to fish, after they had worked all night catching nothing. Following His direction, they did as he suggested and almost swamped their boats with all the fish they caught. "So they brought the boats ashore, left everything and followed him." Luke 5:11. Wow.

If we were called by Jesus to follow Him, would we, could we leave everything behind—jobs, possessions, family—everything that comprises our comfort zone—leave it all and just follow? We would like to say we would, but that's in the abstract, a hypothetical scenario secure in the knowledge that Jesus has been here and is gone, and for all we know, won't be coming back for awhile. So it's easy to say "Yes, we would leave all that we have accumulated over a lifetime and follow a man claiming to be God, with no proof." Yes, in the way of proof, Jesus did perform a miracle by giving them a catch of fish the likes of which they had probably never witnessed before. But out there on the lake, was it a miracle, or were they just great fishermen, and was the fact that this stranger told them to go back out and lower their nets after a night of failure just a coincidence? We tend to take credit for the successes in our lives. To acknowledge the workings of God in our lives and to give Him credit for those good things we experience is not in our nature. So would we, really, leave everything and follow Him?

In our day-to-day living we can program ourselves to give credit to God more than we might, but it is a challenge. Maybe in the days of Peter and his friends their lives were more focused on their faith and on God, or maybe not. The Jews had been waiting for the promised messiah for thousands of years, and so far nothing. Why, all of a sudden, would these men recognize Jesus as the Messiah and follow a new career, a new vocation, if you will, based on some fish? What would it take for us to do the same thing today, in our world, in our time? Only if we make our faith more essential to our lives and to everything we do might we be better able to follow that call if it were to come. In fact, it does come, every day. It may mean to just be nicer to our fellow man, or to refrain from using bad language or cheating on our taxes, trying to be an example to our fellow beings. Maybe it means more prayer—not the rote recital of words, but a real conversation with God about our relationship with Him. It probably means entering into a relationship with Him that would enable us to answer that call in the event that it comes, when it comes. But are we willing to commit to that kind of relationship? As humans we say, "Sure, you bet!", but as Christians, being sinful beings like Simon and Isaiah and Paul, do we not know better about how hard that would be, really? Would we? Could we?

32

The Human Christ

I think there may be the impression among many Christians that the short time between the Last Supper and the Crucifixion was the time of Christ's suffering on earth. Those were the days when the suffering was most visceral, most evident to the world, most recorded for history. But at what time in His life did Jesus really come to understand what would be required of Him? He was born a human baby, and had what we can assume was a normal childhood before he went into business with Joseph. We know He began His public ministry three years before the days of agony he suffered in Jerusalem during that first Holy Week. But at what point during those years from Christmas to His baptism in the Jordan by John did He really understand what He was getting Himself into? He was God as well as man. Did that fact make the baby in the manger already know His destiny? As a little boy, learning to walk and to talk, playing in His home with Mary watching over Him, did He understand who He was and what it was He came to do? Somehow I doubt it. As a human he should have been growing and learning, being cranky sometimes, hungry, getting the flu and maybe the measles, falling down and crying over a skinned knee like any normal little boy. As a young man, a teenager, would He have seen the girl next door and wonder if she was His type?

At what point in His humanity did He recognize His deity? At what point did He understand that His would be a short life, a controversial life, a life unlike any other, that would reconcile man to God through suffering and death. At what point did he understand that if He chose, He could perform miracles? How did He converse with Mary and Joseph regarding these eventualities, and what kind of comfort did He offer them, son to parent, God to man? There is something called the age of reason that one attains at some point in one's growing up that gives one the wisdom and knowledge to know right from wrong, make decisions regarding life and faith. Is that when Jesus came to understand His role on earth, and did that age come to Him at about the same time as other human children? If not I wonder when. Mary understood His power and His destiny based on what the angel had told her before she became pregnant. She knew He would suffer at the hands of evil men. But when did she recognize His power? How long before the wedding feast at Cana when she asked Him to turn water into wine did she see that He was ready? Or was it at that moment that she responded to some inspiration, some whisper from the Spirit that now was the time? And if so, how could she as His mother, shoo Him out the door into public ministry without regret? Maybe it wasn't without regret.

My point is, as both God and Man, the life of Jesus must have been something pretty unusual by our standards. Forget about Holy Week. How does God behave here on earth as a Human without conflict, how does He react to His power, His mission, His impending ministry with all that that entails? How much emotional agony preceded His execution? Yes, as God He must have known what His ultimate goal was and how much pain would be required to achieve that goal. But as Human, as a real child of the human race, how and when did He reconcile His "Godness" with His Humanity? As God He had to know that scourging and crucifixion were in the cards for Him, but as Man how did He agree to go through having nails driven through His hands and feet instead of just continuing to drive nails into wood as a carpenter?

33

Created By God

There was a train of thought being expressed in the sermon this week by my pastor regarding the "Aura of God" present around people who have been baptized, confirmed, etc. insofar as they have been "Created by God, not someone else . . . ." This struck me as a very mistaken way to make a point, whatever that point was. I'm not sure what he was trying to say, but if there is life, then it was created by God. Period. The Church may not approve of all manner in which life comes into being, but that does not exclude the Almighty from ultimate participation in its creation.

Where human sexuality is concerned, my church seems to be very uncomfortable making reference to it, let alone teaching about it with any moral authority. Perhaps this has to do with the fact that the ones making pronouncements regarding sex are themselves unmarried at best and sexually and morally flawed at worst. The Church has taught regarding family planning, birth control, artificial insemination and all manner of procreation and its manageability for centuries, but especially in the past fifty years, since the pill and subsequent fertility issues have been explored. Short of planning when or if a married couple should have sex, the Church leaves little room for any more control over if, when or how many children to bring into the world. Nevertheless, if those pronouncements are disregarded by people and a pregnancy occurs, the baby born is no less a child of God than any other, and to imply from the pulpit that a life can be created without the power of God fundamentally involved in that creation is wrong.

I am of the opinion that once a pregnancy occurs there is life, both before and after delivery, and to terminate that pregnancy, for whatever reason, is morally wrong. However, married couples engaging in sexual activity without the intention of creating life, practicing whatever birth control method they may find appropriate for themselves, should not be judged immoral by the religious authorities that be. If a married couple is infertile, should they be told that it is not appropriate to have sex? If a couple has reached that post-menopausal age when pregnancy is no longer possible under normal circumstances, should they be prohibited from engaging in sexual activity? Yes, in either circumstance, miracles are possible, but the likelihood of having a child is not high. So, should a couple be told not to engage in sex because it is unlikely that their lovemaking will produce a child? Should a couple be told not to have sex if the woman is already pregnant? I don't believe that that was ever the teaching of the Church. If "natural family planning" is acceptable to the Church, trying to have sex only during that time of the month when the woman is not ovulating, is that different than any of the above situations? I don't see how it could be considered so. So how can one method of birth control be acceptable while another is not? If procreation is the only justification for sex, then there should be no sexual activity at all approved of unless it is the intention of the couple to have a child. And if procreation of one kind is acceptable, why is not another? The life created is no less a child of God in any circumstance.

So, how can a life be created by someone other than God? During the same service, the priest blessed the water in anticipation of sprinkling the congregation, and in doing so called upon God "the Creator of ALL life . . ." to bless the water. His personal opinions regarding the morality of one kind of procreation or another fly in the face of this prayer, and should not be expressed from the pulpit as if it were a fundamental truth. In my opinion it is not.

34

Our Core

There was a story on Speaking of Faith this weekend on Alzheimer's Disease. The disease is said to be the most feared of all diseases in this country, more so than heart disease, stroke or even cancer. It is described as "the great un-learning," in that all that we are as the result of experiences and memories acquired during a lifetime are lost as our memory fails. What remains after those memories are lost? It was said that what remains is the core of who we are, who we have always been, but a core that may likely have been camouflaged by those very experiences that made us who we were recognized as having been by our families, friends and peers. Other sensory aspects of our core selves retain traces of memory that our brains have lost. In other words, memory is not simply a single element located in a single part of the body, the brain, but rather has vestiges in our other senses, such as smell and touch and hearing, that survive to a degree even after the brain's contribution to memory is gone.

I have said that it is my belief that who we are is the result of all the experiences of a lifetime, the people we've met, the ones we've loved and hated, the ones we've had and lost, the betrayals of enemies and the loyalty of friends, the lessons learned in school, on the playground and in the office. If all these things that make us who we are are gone, who remains? Are we good or evil, kind or cruel, patient or impatient, tolerant or intolerant? What was fundamental to our nature before the influence of any external experience entered our lives? Are we more similar to one another as created beings, or are we dissimilar? How does the world and the experiences inherent therein change who we started out to be? What talents remain after everything that was learned is unlearned? Do we tend to be people persons or isolated by choice. Do these differences explain a predisposition to prejudice of one kind or another before Alzheimer's? Do we have more an affinity toward faithfulness to the Divine or a susceptibility to rebellion? If we have no memory and are fundamentally who we started out to be, are we still sons of Adam and Eve, or has original sin been cauterized? If we have forgotten a sinful past, are we still responsible for those sinful acts? If all memory of sin is gone, and the inclination to sin no longer exists, are the slates wiped clean, whether we were once God-fearing beings or serial murderers?

If we have unlearned everything that made us recognizable to those around us, would those we have loved and those who have loved us still retain the bond that drew us together in the first place? Do those memories left in sensory places apart from a vacant mind still keep us in contact with one another, whether or not the communication of that bond remains? If both husband and wife are relegated to the nether world of Alzheimer's and both reside in the same physical place, would they find each other and bond anew based on something elemental that was there but maybe not recognized at the beginning of their relationship prior to the onset of the disease? I would hope so.

It was observed that as patients of Alzheimer's we suffer less from the disease than do those loved ones around us. As our memory fades and loved ones become strangers, it is they who recognize the differences in who we are and what remains (and what is missing) while the patient recognizes none of these things. We may be confused at first and troubled at what may be coming, but the disease is relatively benign to its sufferer as it progresses, unlike other illnesses. From this standpoint, those witnesses to the eventual destruction of the personality that was should be less pained by what they see than if their loved one were in physical discomfort. But this is easy to say. Who we love is the personality that is fading, the memories of a lifetime together. It must be like death arrives and we begin to grieve the loss before the breathing stops and the body chills. Death itself may arrive as more of a relief than further grief, because we have already grieved the loss of this loved one, perhaps over a long period of time. Who remains may not be anything like who we remember and loved, so the grief of loss has more to do with that change than the physical separation of death.

I don't know if this disease is in my future or not. Certain aspects of getting older lead us to fear that it may be, but these aspects of the natural aging process are normal to most of us. I hope that I will remember my family and friends until death comes, but if that is not to be, perhaps some comfort may be found in this essay. And perhaps, with as many baby boomers as there are flirting with the aging process, more effort towards finding a treatment or cure will be forthcoming before we arrive at that point. So much the better. But in any event, it's probably okay. Thy will be done.

35

Prayer

I find prayer to be hard to do effectively, at least as I've been taught should be proper prayer. I find my mind wandering during Mass even when I try to concentrate on the words of the worship. To just pray, that's difficult for me, unless there is something specific that I am praying for. Then I find prayer self-serving, more to gain something from God than to simply worship Him with my words and thoughts. If someone or I, myself, am in need I can pray, but to just pray in order to bring myself closer to God is difficult for me. I know that to ask for something from God in prayer is encouraged, but it doesn't seem quite right if I can't just offer my time to Him in a quiet moment with no real personal objective in mind. During worship I try to keep my mind on the words of the service, but I can't stay with it from beginning to end without distraction. But maybe that's just human. Maybe the effort to communicate with God is the most important thing, not that I can't stay with it. And maybe that kind of concentration only comes with repetition and practice. Maybe (no, definitely) I don't save enough time in my day to just say hello to the Almighty, and if I did perhaps I'd be more successful (in my estimation) at establishing easy conversation. Perhaps the prayers of a worship service are intended to make us contemplate things that we don't usually think seriously about, and that is the more important part of prayer, even if that takes our mind on a tangent. To have our mind take us to an unfamiliar place that brings us closer to God is perhaps the whole point of prayer. And perhaps just the quiet time spent in private prayer is, in fact, communication with God, even if no words are spoken. Just quieting oneself, making room for Him and time for Him is prayer, in and of itself. Maybe just quieting myself, in His presence, without the worry of daily distractions and concerns, and not getting so tensed up and frustrated with not accomplishing something that I was taught in second grade was "proper prayer" is the goal. We have enough in life to keep us distracted and worried and pressured about. Maybe just putting that sort of thing out of mind, relaxing and just enjoying being with Him, quiet in His presence, wherever that might be, is in fact "proper prayer".

36

The Blood of Jesus

We have just finished Holy Week, and I've been thinking about something. There was a piece on television a couple of weeks ago about an archaeologist on a quest for some nails reported to have been buried in the tomb of the high priest, Caiaphas. His suspicion was that they were nails from the crucifixion of Jesus. Although they were reported in the archaeological paperwork describing what the original discoverers found in the tomb of Caiaphas, there were no photographs of them and none were found in the tomb with him. It got me thinking about what he would have found if the nails were there.

The Crucifixion was a violent, bloody affair, as were the events leading up to the actual crucifixion. All four Gospels refer to the suffering and ultimate death of Jesus. In Chapter 27 Matthew refers to the scourging, the crowning of thorns, the soldiers clothing Jesus in a military cloak and mocking Him, the crucifixion and the burial linens He was wrapped in when they placed Him in the tomb. In Chapter 15 Mark, too, refers to the scourging, the crowning of thorns, the soldiers clothing Jesus in "royal purple", the crucifixion and the linen burial shroud. In his Chapter 22 Luke talks of Jesus suffering in Gethsemane and great drops of blood falling as He prayed to His Father. In Chapter 23 he speaks of the crucifixion and the fine linen He was wrapped in for burial. John 19 describes the scourging, the crucifixion, the soldier piercing His side after He died, water and blood flowing from His body, and of the burial wrappings.

During Lent our bible study group watched Mel Gibson's "The Passion of the Christ." It is a graphic portrayal of all of the above—the brutality of the scourging and of the crucifixion, with blood left on the ground during the scourging, the blood flowing from Jesus' brow after they placed the crown of thorns on His head, the nails being driven into His hands and feet on the cross. During all that took place, blood was shed—on the ground, on the cloak He wore when they mocked Him, on the thorns they placed on His head, on the nails and on the wood of the cross. They wrapped His body in burial linen, perhaps bloody or perhaps cleaned (if they had time before the beginning of the sabbath), and placed Him in the tomb.

Now, even if you find Gibson's depiction of the passion over the top, the fact is that punishment and the death penalty in those times involved violence and was a bloody course of events. My point is not whether blood was shed, for that is undeniable. My question is, after the resurrection, did the blood remain? Yes, they probably cleaned up the area where they scourged Him after the fact, but even the bloody water had to be disposed of somewhere. Someone owned the cloak or even the "royal purple", whatever that may have been. Blood undoubtedly remained on the garment as a result of the scourging. He wasn't buried with the crown of thorns still on His head. Where did the crown go? His wounded body must have left blood on the nails and on the cross. And the linens. They were left at the tomb. Were they still bloody when discovered by the disciples? Some evidence of the suffering had to have remained behind under normal circumstances, (though these were anything but normal circumstances.) Some of His DNA had to have been deposited—on the ground, on the whips, on the cloak, on the thorns, on the cross and on the burial linen. And speaking of His DNA, what did it contain? He was fully man, born of Mary. He had to have had her family's DNA included in His own, dating back to King David. But what of His Father? Does divinity have DNA? Somehow I doubt it. So what then represented His Paternal lineage in His DNA?

My thoughts run to the resurrection. He rose from the dead. He spent time with his disciples. He ascended to Heaven. My question then is, did He leave any of His human, physical self behind? Or at the point of resurrection, did He become whole, unscourged and uncrowned. We know that His wounds remained, or Thomas would have had no proof to dispel his doubts. But when He ascended, did He ascend to Heaven with all the humanity He came with, or did He leave something behind. And if so where, and in what form?

37

An Adult Examination of Faith

I realize that it probably isn't realistic, but it seems to me that an adult examination of oneself is a valuable if a scary prospect. We send our children to Sunday School and Catechism in order to teach them about the faith we proclaim to hold as our own, from the time they are pre-schoolers on through high school, in one form or another. That's good. They need to know what it's about, worshipping together as a family, saying certain prayers, observing certain rituals and holidays. As children they need to be taught something about faith and religion and a relationship with God. The faith and the religion they are taught are ours. As adults they should be thinking for themselves and coming to their own conclusions as to what it is that they believe, who it is that they are, what is their relationship with God.

In recent years I have begun to take this examination more seriously than I did as a young man. I have considered the things I was taught as a child and decided which of those things I really considered as part of my own faith, not my parents' faith. I came to the conclusion that I am not a textbook Catholic, but I am closer to being Catholic than anything else. It has been said that when we accept someone else's teachings as our own, we must accept the errors in those teachings as well as the truths. Only by examining the faith we have been taught as a thinking adult and forming a considered faith of our own can we be true to ourselves and to our God.

So each person should examine his or her own faith and determine for oneself what that faith consists of. Is it the faith of our parents or has it evolved over a lifetime? In order to be true to ourselves and to our God, we must at least examine what it is that we believe. And we must know what it is that we believe in order to find our way along the path where we seek to find God. We have recently accepted a revision of the Liturgy of the Mass, a closer translation to the original Latin. In experiencing the new words said by the priest and by ourselves, we must pay attention to what is said and what it all means. We can no longer just coast along without thinking about what's happening at the altar. Our faith deserves just such an examination.

38

Theology

Theology has been considered by many, at least by theologians, as one monolithic entity, universal and beyond question or challenge. But it depends on which theologian you talk to. One man's theology is another man's heresy. Theology is defined as "The study of the nature of God and religious belief." But how you define that nature and that belief determines the theology of which you speak.

There are as many theologies in the world as there are religions. If that were not the case, there would be only one theology, one religion and one human understanding of the Deity. As it is each religious belief has its own determination as to what theology ultimately is. Each will argue the merits of its own and the error of the other theologies that exist. Between every major (and minor) religion in the world, there are disagreements as to the nature of God and how to achieve salvation (or reincarnation, or whatever reward/punishment each contemplates.) And even within different religions, Christianity, Judaism, Islam—whichever religion you wish to discuss—each has its divisions and disagreements, judgments for and against, even physical violence and, at times, death against those within that same religion that hold a different interpretation of God, or variant "theology".

My experience has been with the Roman Catholic church and its theology, both pre—and post-Vatican Council. Yet there are other Catholics—Orthodox, Coptic, Tridentine and others—that have theologies similar yet different from Rome. I have been exposed to Lutheran theology from my wife and family and have found that there are differences in theology between the two bodies of faith, but more similarities than differences.

My point is, to what extent do we trust others as to the truth or falseness of any one theology as opposed to determining for oneself what is accurate for each of us? I have said earlier that if we accept someone else's interpretation of what is right, we must also accept whatever errors may be inherent in that interpretation. To what extent will we be judged for whatever theology we finally claim as our own, or will it be the honest search for truth that is most valuable to the God that each theology claims as its own? There are things that we will never understand about the God we worship, simply because He is God. Does anyone, theologian or not, really have a handle on "the nature of God" or what is the right "religious belief" system? We cling to a theology because it gives us security, because it is what we were raised with, because it was what we became converted to believe in. We cling to the hope that the belief system we claim as our own is the one that will take us home to paradise. Do we need to fear that that belief system is wrong, or is the attempt the thing that will take us there?

If we are indeed serious and dutiful about the search for God and for salvation, will we be condemned for adhering to the wrong theology? Each theology claims that the Bible speaks for them on the issue, and that their own interpretation of Scripture proves that their own position as the right one. But is any theology that monolithic entity that each one claims to be, and can any study of God by humans be entirely without error?

39

Mother Mary

Mary holds a remarkable place in history. As the Mother of God she is probably the second most honored person since the Creation, after her Son. I am not a person who spends a lot of time praying for her intercession, I don't say the rosary, I don't have a Marian statue in my garden or on my dash. I don't not honor her, but she is not the center of my faith as it seems she may be for some, especially in certain cultures. And yet she is an interesting person in history, especially Christian history.

As a young woman she was approached to be the Mother of Jesus, the Christ. She accepted that role and was warned that there would be pain involved, not just the physical pain of childbirth, but the emotional pain inherent in the life of her Son. She agreed, nevertheless. But I wonder if she could have known what was ahead of her at such a tender age.

As a parent and as a grandparent, I am aware of the pain of watching your children grow and become independent. We see them hurt, physically when they fall down, and emotionally when they are picked on or when things don't go as fairly as they and we would like. We don't know exactly what kind of childhood Jesus had. Was it pretty normal for a young Jewish boy in those days, or was it special as God's Son, subject to more or less of the same kinds of pain and anguish—and laughter—as other children of the era? And what of Mary's view of all this?

In John's gospel account of the crucifixion, we are told that Mary was at the cross at the time of His suffering and death. We know that she was witness to some of His miracles, in fact she instigated His first miracle at the wedding feast at Cana. She saw Him teach at the temple as a young Boy. But what was her life like, knowing the role He would play and the pain He would suffer? Or did she fully understand it all? At what point in life did she begin to agonize as a mother about the pain He would have to go through. And what about after His death?

My sister died at a young age, and I know my mother never got over it. She suffered the pain of that loss until the day she died. What about Mary? We don't have much information about her after His ascension and the Pentecost. The Church assumes that she was carried to Heaven after she died, but for someone as honored and revered by as many as there have been in history, we don't really know much about how she dealt with the birth, life, death and aftermath of a her Son. Surely the agony of witnessing the suffering and death of Jesus was terrible, regardless of how much she may have understood and accepted the need for that ordeal for humankind. As a human mother it had to have caused her deep suffering.

So my question is, as a human mother of a human and divine Son, how did she handle it? She is honored because of her role as the Mother of God, but we don't often think about how that role of mother (small "m") affected her personally. I am sure that she understood, at least after the fact, the role her Son played in the salvation of the world, and knew that He returned from where He came, to the right hand of His Father in Heaven. I'm sure that she was happy to have been privileged to have played the important role that she did. As a young Jewish woman she knew the prophets had predicted what she had been a part of and had to be thankful for the result of that work. But even with that knowledge, at what cost to her, personally?

40

Faith in a Citizenship in Heaven

We'd like to believe that we are knowledgeable about all things in space and time. However, depending on who you talk to, those beliefs are varied and at odds with one another. There was a time when man believed that the world was flat. That was proved not to be the case. There was a time when man and the Christian religion believed that the earth was the center of the universe and that the sun and all the stars and planets revolved around it. Galileo even underwent prosecution and imprisonment during the Inquisition for his support of a different view, so strongly did the Church and most religious authorities of the time feel about the subject. Even recently scientists have found some evidence that the universe is expanding and accelerating in that expansion rather than contracting as has been believed since Einstein's theory of relativity was espoused.

In short our understanding of the universe and its creation and ultimate destination are unknowable given the information we have. Each new discovery lends additional evidence to our limited grasp of creation, but no real knowledge. And yet, as Christians, we believe. We believe in the creation story in Genesis. We don't understand how evidence of prehistoric beings—animal, vegetable and human—correlate with the first book of the Bible, but we have faith, nevertheless.

And so we come to Philippians. We are told by Paul of our future as citizens of Heaven and of glorious bodies like that of Jesus. Is faith in this prophesy any less probable than a belief that God created the heavens and the earth out of nothing? Do we believe that Jesus was the Son of God and that as man, he died as a sacrifice for the sins of men? This is the premise upon which the entire faith of Christianity is based. Without that faith there is no Christianity. Whether Einstein was correct or not, whether recent discoveries are correct or not, regardless of what we believe about our creation and the condition of that creation, both now and in eternity, if we believe in the basis for Christianity then having faith in a citizenship in Heaven when the final judgement comes is not so far-fetched. Faith is just that—a belief in something we can't prove, but believe nevertheless. Having faith in God, the Father, the Son and the Spirit, leads us to have faith in all that He promises, including salvation for eternity in a place called Heaven or in a body called glorious by Paul or just in an existence we don't understand any more than we understand the physical phenomenon we call the universe. Faith is confidence in the reality of things we can't prove as humans, and ultimately that's what Christianity amounts to.

41

Three Wise Men

There are in the Old Testament prophesies of the coming of a Messiah. They predate the Nativity by thousands of years in some cases. They describe the birth coming to a virgin and they say it will happen in Bethlehem in Judea. But nowhere does it say when the birth will occur.

Now comes the Gospel of Matthew. Three kings arrive in Jerusalem at the palace of Herod. They were obviously important enough in appearance to have been granted an audience with him. They were asking where they might find the new-born King of the Jews. They say they had seen His star rising in the East and had come to pay Him homage. Now, we can assume that the shepherds that heard the angelic announcement of the birth of Jesus, who had gone to the stable to witness the event that had been foretold were Jews. We can also assume that these wise men, astronomers from the East were not Jews. They probably had read the Jewish prophesies if they were learned men and were interested in such things. But what made them think that the star that they had witnessed rising was the star of Jesus? What made them think that this Jesus was the promised King of the Jews, and believe it to such an extent that they would each undertake such a journey? A journey on camels, of an unknown distance, that would take them away from home for who knew how long a time? They knew something unique. How is it that no one in the Roman Empire was as well-educated and knowledgeable enough of the peoples whose lands they occupied to have the same information? The Roman Empire must have been advanced enough to have astronomers and students of history and theology who would, under the same circumstances, at least have inquired about this new star and its meaning. Was the star visible in middle eastern skies before it shown down on the stable? And how is it that of all the stars in the sky, this one would have led men on a journey? And how would one riding on a camel be able to follow its path to a specific latitude and longitude to find a stable out in the pastures of Bethlehem and then stop them at a specific spot where they might find sheep and oxen, but certainly not a new-born king?

We are told that they are warned in a dream not to return to Herod when they left for home. I think that they may have been inspired by dreams or angels or something to undertake this adventure. I think there must be much to the story that the gospel writers didn't put in their accounts. That is probably not unusual, because just looking at the differences in the four gospels, it is apparent that each had his own way of looking at the accounts of the life of Jesus. Each told of different events, some of the same events, some longer and some shorter than the others. We have been told all that is necessary to know about these gentiles who were favored with inclusion in the Christmas story. They have been standard characters for two thousand years, to the point that we don't really think much about them except that they were "wise men" who arrived at the stable with gifts—important gifts, fit for a King. Gifts that had been foretold by Isaiah many, many years before. We kind of take them for granted as just part of the story. Three more visitors that greeted Mary and Joseph and the Baby, along with shepherds and animals and angels. Different characters than the others, but still, just part of a familiar story.

I think that there is much more to find out about these remarkable men—aliens, really, in a story that had been told for the Jews, but now a story for all mankind. And the star—a light shining in the darkness. There was something very special about the whole story of these three Maji. More than we're told.

42

Grace Differences

B elief in grace is different between Catholics and Protestants, at least as most understand it to be. "Catholic doctrine teaches that God uses the sacraments to facilitate the reception of His grace." Charles C. Ryrie, *The Grace of God* (Chicago: Moody Press, 1963), pp 10-11 "Protestants generally do not hold that view." Saint Aquinas. Justification by Grace. "In other words, even without the sacraments, divine grace has been imparted by God to humanity." http://www.experiencefestival.com/a/ Heaven_-_Heaven_in_Protestant_Christianity.

Protestants believe that grace is bestowed to all, as a result of Jesus having died on the cross as a sacrifice for the sins of man. Some d enominations believe that grace is finite, as is the number of people who will be allowed into Heaven after the Judgement. I don't believe that. Thomas Aquinas taught that grace is somehow a physical entity, bestowed on believers in increments through the reception of the sacraments, and therefore, by implication, a finite quantity. I don't believe that, either. I don't believe that grace is any more a physical substance than is thought or belief or prayer, and therefore has no limit to its abundance.

As a Catholic I believe that grace is available to all people, to accept or to reject, and acceptance is a result of penitence. I believe that acceptance or rejection is the only difference between salvation and damnation. But rejecting the grace of God is a choice we make as sinful beings. We make certain choices for behavior in our lives, both good and bad, but they are our choices. Being perfect people is not possible given our history from Eden on. But that is not to say that trying to be as perfect as we can be, trying to obey God's law, trying to treat one another as we would like to be treated, prayer to God, honoring Him as all-powerful and all-merciful is unnecessary. This attempt throughout life makes those attempts more of a habitual behavior, successful or not, and makes grace and salvation all the more likely at the end of our life here on earth. To behave as if there is plenty of time to convert, no consequence for our behavior, no need to worry about the sins we commit, is to risk not having the ability or the humility to accept God's grace at the end.

Grace is, by definition, a free gift. It is given by God to mankind. We say in our creeds that we deserve temporal and eternal punishment for our sins. We believe that, but we also believe that forgiveness and salvation are ours as well, if only we accept the gift. Adam and Eve sinned. They were kicked out of Eden for their sin and all that was easy about their life before was no longer easy. We inherited original sin from them, but forgiven by the sacrament of Baptism. We have personally sinned as well, from the time we were old enough to be aware of the difference between right and wrong until the time we die. That's a given. But if we accept the gift (and doing so is easier if we try), the rest is already accomplished on our behalf.

43

Capital Punishment

Mankind has been executing criminals for most of recorded history by one means or another—stoning, burning at the stake, beheading, hanging, firing squad, electrocution, lethal injection—what have you. And crucifixion. I have heard ministers refer to the outstretched arms of Christ on the cross as a sign welcoming mankind to salvation. I suspect that there is little coincidence in the workings of God. I wonder if this particular form of capital punishment became the norm at this particular time in human history for that very specific reason? Jesus could have been killed by any means, but it may have been difficult to make an allegorical comparison with most other forms of execution. As inhumane as it was, cruel and unusual, if you will, crucifixion may very well have been planned to send that very sign of "Welcome" to a mankind awaiting salvation.

44

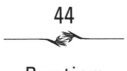

Baptism

There was an article the other day regarding an elderly Frenchman who was raised Catholic in a very strict, very conservative village in northwest France. As he grew to adulthood, he became acquainted with a group of "Free Thinkers." He became an atheist and requested that the Church delete him from their records. They sent him a copy of his baptismal record and noted in the margin that he had chosen to leave the Church. Some years later he decided to take it further and requested that the Church "de-baptize" him. The priest told him that this was not possible and he sued the Church.

The dean of Canon Law at the Catholic University of America said that it is impossible to be de-baptized because baptism changes one permanently before God and the Church. "One could refuse the grace offered by God, the grace offered by the sacrament, refuse to participate, but we would believe the individual has still been marked for God through the sacrament, and that individual at any point could return to church."

I'm not sure why a believer would stop believing, but that's beside the point. Even if you wished to be removed from the rolls of the Church, how important is it to go to the trouble of being "de-baptized"? If you don't believe, why is that part of your religious history so objectionable? If you don't believe in God, don't believe in the sacrament of Baptism and have been removed from the Church's roster of members, how does the "removal" of the sacrament, even if it were possible, make a difference. It sounds like someone wanting to make a public point about his decisions regarding God and religion. A true atheist doesn't believe in God or the sacraments of the Church. So if that belief (or lack thereof) is valid for him, the original ceremony of the sacrament shouldn't be regarded as anything of consequence. So why make an issue when for him no issue really exists?

But regarding the sacrament of Baptism, it does make a difference to the human soul. It removes original sin and any other sins that may have been committed by the one receiving the sacrament prior to reception. It makes one "a child of God" in a very real and indelible sense, even though that reality isn't a visible sign of grace. It exists nevertheless. Say someone were immunized against a certain disease, like polio as an example, and later in life discovered that there may be something beneficial to not have been inoculated." Perhaps not having been immunized would make someone less likely to develop Alzheimer's disease, for instance. If one were less afraid of getting polio than of contracting Alzheimer's could one be "de-immunized?" Of course not. That's a rather crass analogy, but my point is that once one has had something indelible done, making it not indelible and removing it and its effects is no longer possible. If, as we believe, that Baptism removes sin, then do we get the sin back because of de-baptism? We may get a different sin as the result of the wish or the attempt, but the original sin is gone, never again to be incurred. We are sinful beings, but that's one sin we, ourselves, cannot commit, and once it's been washed away by the water and the word, it's gone forever. And if the individual ever sees the error of his ways and wishes to return to full communion, Baptism is not necessary for that reconciliation. Once is sufficient.

45

Different Views of God

Recently I have heard a couple of men, both priests, give opinions on how many of us Catholics view God. One was by Fr. Ron Rolheiser regarding how his having grown up in the Church of the fifties, the Baltimore Catechism, the Latin Mass and a generally conservative religion has affected his life as an adult Catholic and a priest. We regarded Roman Catholicism as the only "true" Christian religion and viewed other denominations as lesser Christians who would have difficulty attaining salvation, but rather would probably spend eternity in a place called Limbo. We were discouraged from even attending their services. That attitude has changed, as Fr. Rolheiser explained in his essay.

Again, this past Saturday a visiting priest saying Mass talked of how many of us view God as Someone who would cause destruction in the world, like 9/11, Hurricane Katrina, the earthquake in Haiti, etc. as punishment for sinfulness in our lives and in the life of the world. He challenged anyone to find anything in the Scriptures that would indicate that He is anything but a loving and a forgiving God, not One who would destroy lives as punishment. Anyone who has the view of God as anything but loving and forgiving needs to reevaluate his or her perception of the God we worship.

Many Catholics, especially the ones who grew up prior to Vatican II, probably struggle with their feelings about the God that we learned about in catechism as opposed to the One described currently. Now we are encouraged to recognize One who sees all men and women as members of His flock, equally deserving of His grace and mercy, and, as a result, His salvation. I don't know about non-Catholics and their opinions of others, but based on my own personal observations I suspect that many may struggle with those same issues. The Catholicism of my youth was kind of an Old Testament religion in the sense that God was frightful and distant. The priest was the only one authorized to touch the Sacrament with his hands, only the wafer was received in Communion, placed on the tongue by the priest, and most of the Mass was foreign to the parishioners except as they followed the English translation in their missals as the priest said the entire Mass in Latin. There was no question about the salvation gained through Christ's crucifixion, but that deserving salvation was questionable at best, given humanity's sinful nature. There would assuredly be a lot of time spent in purgatory, assuming we were faithful enough to attain Heaven eventually. The clergy were beyond reproach, and to question their directives was in itself sinful. We never heard of the priest's human failings, rarely saw him outside of church services and never really got to know him personally. Not so anymore.

The God we learned about in catechism from some intimidating and seemingly unhappy nuns was a God of reproach, not approach. In reading the Book of Job it seems that Job's situation was somewhat like our own, though maybe a bit more severe. Now, remember, these are memories of a 1950's youngster, intimidated by those who taught with the same severity that they probably felt as clergy and nuns. Looking back over half a century these may have been impressions that were not entirely accurate. Perhaps these intimidating and seemingly unhappy nuns were completely satisfied with their lives back at the convent among fellow nuns, laughing, joking but still prayerful and at peace with the decision they had made as young women to devote themselves to this vocation. The clergy may have been less happy. Given their isolation from most of their parishioners and other priests, it may have been quite a lonely vocation to have to live out. They had the respect of their parishioners, and the authority to hand down orders to be followed without much discussion, but at what point do these "perks" lose their importance in the face of a lifetime of aloneness?

But getting back to our view of God. In my opinion, God is very approachable. We can talk to Him, either in formal prayer or simply in silence, thankful for the graces we have been given and asking for help in times of trial. We can see Him, both in the splendor of the universe and in the might of an erupting volcano, in waves crashing on a beach, in a sunset or on a quiet lake. Depending on how we see Him, when we got to know Him, these different views may have very different effects on different people. Awesome fear or awesome beauty. If we see the former, it's unfortunate. If we see the latter, we are blessed. If we go to Mass because we've been warned that to not is to commit mortal sin and risk eternal damnation, we miss the point. If we go because we appreciate the beauty of the ceremony and the chance to meet Him personally, we are blessed. If our religion and our faith are based on fear, life is a lonely journey. If they are based on a confidence in salvation and in the realization that Jesus, the Divine became one like us, saw those same waves and sunsets and star-filled skies and appreciated their beauty, we are blessed. Old-time religion or a newer, fresher look at the Divine. I've seen it from both vantages, and the blessedness of the fresh look is far more satisfying than the scarier version of my youth. Just one man's opinion.

*   *   *

As a very young man I spent two and a half years in a minor seminary, St. John Vianney in Elkhorn, Nebraska. It was associated with a Benedictine monastery there, Mount Michael. St. John's is no longer there as a seminary, but has been replaced by Mount Michael High School, and Mount Michael Monastery is now Mount Michael Abbey. But it is still of the Benedictine order. Those two and a half years had a large impact on me.

If you read the Rule of St. Benedict, the first word in his rule is "Listen." The first line starts, "Listen carefully, my child, to your master's precepts, and incline the ear of your heart . . . ." It is from Proverbs 4:20.

If we are true to our faith, whatever that faith is, the most important thing is to listen—to God, to His word, His instruction, His revealed message for us personally. I don't want to be seen as something special, some seer of God's truth for mankind. That's not what this has been about. I can't just sit down and write an essay at will. But there are occasions when something comes to mind that requires me to write down my thoughts. I believe this is listening to God. It isn't necessarily profound revelation, just thoughts that need further introspection. They aren't intended to be masterworks or a new epistle for the faithful. They are mine. If you'd like to, I'm happy to share them, but ideally you should be listening for your own inspiration. Listen. God speaks to each of us personally, uniquely, speaking to our own needs. Listen. If these essays have helped open your mind to the possibility of asking questions, not about the veracity of the revealed Word of the Scriptures, but about how we see our relationship with God and how we find our way home, I'm glad. If they bore you, that's okay, too. I'm not trying to convert anyone to anything, but rather to merely listen. If we all listen to God the world will be better for it. But we must listen. His proclamations aren't shouted from the mountaintops, but rather whispered in the recesses of our quiet moments. So try to find more quiet moments in your life and let Him approach you, attentive, listening, open. That is where He finds us, and we find Him.

Made in United States
Orlando, FL
17 March 2022

15895258R00059